Recruiting, Assessing and Supporting Lesbian and Gay Carers and Adopters

A good practice guide for social workers

Gerald P. Mallon

Bridget Betts

BAAF
ADOPTION
& FOSTERING

Published by
**British Association for Adoption & Fostering
(BAAF)**
Skyline House
200 Union Street
London SE1 0LX
www.baaf.org.uk

Charity Registration 275689

British Library Cataloguing in Publication Data
A catalogue record for this book is available from the
British Library

ISBN 1 903699 83 5

Designed by Andrew Haig & Associates
Photographs on cover posed by models
from Digitalvision
Typeset and printed in Great Britain by Aldgate Press

Contents

1 **Introduction** 1
Gay and lesbian fostering and adoption 1
What *is* a family? 2
Conclusion 2

2 **Lesbian and gay identity** 4
The image and demography of the lesbian and gay population 4
Terminology 4
    Sex, gender and sexuality 4
    Sexual orientation 5
Common questions and presumptions 7
Coming out and self-identity 10
    Internalised homophobia 10
Conclusion 11

3 **The legal context** 12
The criminalisation of gay sex 12
    Victorian legislation 12
    Twentieth-century legislation 12
Age of consent 13
Family life and parenting 13
    England and Wales 14
    Scotland 16
    Northern Ireland 16
    National Minimum Standards 16
    Human Rights Act 16
    Section 28 16
    Civil partnership 17
    Unequal sharing of parental responsibility 17

4 **Research on lesbian and gay parenting** 20
Research limitations 20
Fears about lesbian and gay parents 20
Quality of family relations 21
Becoming a parent: making decisions 22
Future research 22
Conclusion 22

5 **Issues for lesbians and gay men when considering parenting** 25
Decision to explore parenting 25
Choosing adoption and fostering 26
Dealing with family of origin issues 27

6   Recruiting lesbian and gay foster carers and adopters   29

   What works in recruitment?   29
        Word of mouth   30
        Use of the press   30
   Agency response to the initial enquiry   30
        Information packs   31
   Specific recruitment of lesbian and gay carers: points to consider   31
   Preparing for negative feedback   31
   Key points   32

7   Assessment of lesbian and gay foster carers and adopters   33

   The challenge for professionals   33
   The assessment process   33
        The concept of competence   34
        A framework for assessment   34
   The first contact   35
   Preparation groups   36
   Referees   36
   The home study   36
   Specific areas to be addressed   37
   Partnerships and relationships   38
        Other adult members of the household   39
        Motivation   39
        Lifestyle   39
        Valuing difference   39
   Safe caring   39
   The child in placement   39
   Panel   40
   Matching and placement   40
   Key points   41

8   Supporting lesbian and gay foster carers and adopters   42

   Informal support   42
   Specific post-placement support issues for lesbian and gay adopters and carers 42
   Characteristics of post-placement and adoption support services   43
   Key points   44

   Useful organisations   45

   Bibliography   47

Acknowledgements

We would like to thank the following for their time and advice: members of the Lesbian and Gay Foster and Adoptive Parents Network (LAGFAPN) and the Northern Support Group and other gay and lesbian carers who have contacted us from all over the country to share their experiences. Thanks also to managers, social workers and carers at Tower Hamlets Family Placement Team, and in particular, Namita Singh.

Thanks also to Richard McKendrick (Director of the Albert Kennedy Trust), Stephen Hicks, Helen Cosis-Brown, Howard Delmonte (PACE) and Alan Burnell (Family Futures) for their time and invaluable advice; Dr Kathryn Morris-Roberts, Dr Perlita Harris, Felicity Collier and Barbara Hutchinson for their comments on the manuscript; and John Simmonds and Mary Lane for their input.

We are grateful to BAAF for agreeing to publish this book, and we are especially appreciative of Shaila Shah, Director of Publications, for her support and assistance.

Note about the authors

Gerald P. Mallon

Gerald P. Mallon, DSW, is Professor and Executive Director of the National Resource Center for Family-Centered Practice and Permanency Planning at the Hunter College School of Social Work in New York City. For more than 29 years, Dr Mallon has been a child welfare practitioner, advocate, researcher, and educator. He is the author or editor of 17 books and numerous peer-reviewed papers in professional journals. His most recent publication from Columbia University Press is *Gay Men Choosing Parenthood*. Dr Mallon earned his doctorate in Social Welfare from the City University of New York at Hunter College and holds an MSW from Fordham University, New York, and a BSW from Dominican College, Blauvelt, NY. He can be reached via email at gmallon@hunter.cuny.edu.

Bridget Betts

Bridget Betts qualified in 1980, and she has held a variety of posts in both the statutory and voluntary sectors during the course of her career. Bridget has worked in the field of adoption and fostering for the past fifteen years, and her role has included the training and preparation of carers and the preparation of children for permanence and adoption, including the completion of life story work. Bridget brings to this area of work her own experience as an adopted person. Since April 1999, Bridget has worked as an independent social worker; she currently works on a freelance basis as a trainer and consultant for a number of agencies. Bridget has produced three interactive CDs for use with children – *My Life Story* offers the opportunity for children and young people to explore who they are, and their feelings about their past, present and the future using an interactive approach. *Speakeasy* is an interactive CD which enables children and young people to express their opinions, wishes and feelings as part of the statutory review process. *Bridget's Taking a Long Time: A journey through adoption from the perspective of a birth child* is an interactive story to help birth children explore the issues involved in adoption; it also includes worksheets and video interviews with birth children. She is currently working on two new interactive resources for children. Bridget can be contacted at bridgetbetts@hotmail.com.

1 Introduction

This book is an attempt to provide social work practitioners with good practice guidelines for working with lesbian and gay foster carers and adopters.

For many lesbians and gay men who are considering parenthood, adoption or fostering is their first choice, but they have often been regarded as a "last resort" by family placement agencies. Although there are a growing number of lesbians and gay men who are applying to adopt or foster, or are successfully caring for children, they remain an under-used resource. With a national shortfall of adoptive and foster placements, agencies need to ensure that they do not deter lesbian and gay applicants from coming forward as potential carers – and that they work effectively and successfully to assess and support gay and lesbian adopters and carers.

In the following chapters we:

- look at lesbian and gay identities;

- examine how the development of policy and legislation has affected the lives of gay men and lesbians and influenced perceptions of them as parents and carers;

- explore the stereotypes, myths and prejudices that influence attitudes towards lesbians and gay men, and particularly to them as carers and parents;

- provide an overview of relevant research on lesbian and gay parenting;

- explore ways of recruiting lesbians and gay men as adopters and foster carers;

- consider issues of best practice at all stages of the assessment process;

- explore ways in which social workers can support lesbian and gay adopters and carers more effectively; and

- signpost further resources and references.

Gay and lesbian fostering and adoption

More than six years ago, Stephen Hicks and Janet McDermott reminded us that 'Lesbians and gay men have always been involved in having and raising children' (1999, p.147). *Lesbian and Gay Fostering and Adoption: Extraordinary yet ordinary* was one of the first books to focus on the experiences of lesbian and gay carers in the UK, telling their stories first-hand and highlighting the issues that face adoption and fostering agencies in positively responding to them as potential carers and valuing them as a resource. It is important for us as co-authors of this guide to acknowledge the influence that Hicks and McDermott's text has had on our thinking and practice, and in the development of this publication. Our work is inspired by, and yet different from, that seminal work.

Lesbians and gay men in the UK have created families in a wide variety of ways, including through adoption, foster care and the establishment of kinship networks. In some cases, lesbians and gay men have become parents or carers without disclosure or discussion of their sexual orientation with adoption and fostering agencies. However, as many lesbians and gay men have become able to live their lives more openly, a greater number are considering parenthood in ways that might not have been thought possible in the past.

For many lesbians and gay men, as pointed out by Hicks and McDermott (1999, p.148), fostering or adoption is not a second choice, as it may be for heterosexual men and women who are infertile (Turner, 1999), but rather a first choice. Lesbians and gay men represent an untapped resource of potential carers for some of the many children who need substitute families. Although lesbians and gay men may have been historically discouraged from fostering or adoption, changes in legislation and policy over the past ten years reflect a more open attitude towards them as parents and carers.

Experiences with social workers, both positive and negative, were well documented in the narratives collected by Hicks and McDermott (1999). The findings from this qualitative work suggest that the social work response to lesbian and gay applicants is varied and unpredictable. Not all social workers are homophobic and some may not be intentionally so; however, a major issue seems to be the lack of policies to guide their practice. Going out on a limb to approve or work with a lesbian or gay carer seemed to be a common theme in these narratives. Also, there were often inconsistencies between or within agencies in the way they responded to lesbian or gay applicants.

It is important that agencies and social workers are prepared for the issues that will arise, both within the agency and individually, in working with lesbian or gay carers. Professionals need to be aware of inaccurate assumptions and stereotypes that have previously shaped legislation and policy and informed practice. Social workers need to examine their own attitudes towards lesbians and gay men. They need to be careful not to assume parenting skills in heterosexual applicants, just as they need to be careful not to assume unsuitability for parenting in lesbian or gay applicants. The sexual orientation of a potential carer does not, of itself, indicate anything about her/his ability to care for children who may have had difficult experiences. Social workers need to explore openly with each individual their experience and skills in relation to caring for a child.

Two issues were identified in Hicks and McDermott's book (1999) as having a negative effect on the assessment process for lesbians and gay men. These were:

- a lack of reliable information about the lives of lesbians and gay men, and

- being defined by one's sexual orientation as a sole aspect of identity.

Acknowledging that specific issues arise for lesbian and gay applicants and dealing with them appropriately are an important part of assessment and ongoing support.

What *is* a family?

Many people, including some social work professionals, are uncomfortable with discussing the idea of gay men and lesbians fostering or adopting children – the issue continues to evoke controversy and strong feelings.

Contemporary public debates about what constitutes a "proper" family can be put into context by considering some of the historical precedents and preconditions to these ideas. Deborah Chambers explores these themes in her book *Representing the Family* (2001). She observes that:

The family was vital to the historical formulation of nationhood and colonial expansion at the level of ideas and structures in nineteenth-century Britain and continues to act as a powerful metaphor and cultural institution for fixing ideas about identity today. It has come to stand for moral order in the public sphere, which is one of the reasons why it is fought over with both such relish and such bitterness in the context of political rhetoric, the news media and public welfare policies. (p.165)

According to Chambers, it is misleading to suggest that the traditional nuclear family is declining or no longer exists:

On the one hand, it has only ever existed as a transitional phase of some people's lives. A variety of living arrangements are being experienced in western nations, including some complex multi-occupancy households that have not, as yet, been given a satisfactory label. On the other hand, the modern nuclear family does exist and is flourishing as an ideal: as a symbol, discourse and powerful myth within the collective imagination. (p.1)

Family structures in the UK, according to BAAF Practice Note 44 (BAAF, 2003a), have become increasingly varied. In 1972 only seven per cent of children were living with a single parent, but by 1998/99 this figure had risen to 23 per cent. In the same period, the number of divorces rose to over 158,700. In 1997, eight per cent of families with dependent children were stepfamilies.

Child placement practice, however, has been cautious in reflecting this increased diversity in family life. Berridge's (1997) research review concluded that only 12 per cent of foster carers were single carers; however, Waterhouse and Brocklesby (2001) in their study of five English local authorities found that 45 per cent of foster carers were single carers. In 1998/99, only five per cent of English adopters were single people (Ivaldi, 2000), although it is widely believed that this has now increased.

Conclusion

Fostering and adoption by lesbians and gay men challenge the traditional notions of family and, in turn, challenge practitioners to examine their own views of what constitutes a family. We would not argue that all lesbians and gay men should be adoptive or foster carers. In the same way, we would never argue that all heterosexuals would make suitable adoptive or foster carers.

In the chapters that follow, we review the research, the relevant legislation and policy, and provide some practical guidance for those conducting assessments and working with lesbian and gay foster and adoptive families. In meeting the needs of the children who are waiting for placements, agencies must explore all potential resources for these children including lesbians and gay men who wish to parent.

2 Lesbian and gay identity

This chapter looks at:

- the image and demography of the lesbian and gay population;
- terminology;
- common questions and presumptions about gay men and lesbians;
- coming out, and lesbian and gay identity.

The image and demography of the lesbian and gay population

It is inaccurate to talk about a lesbian and gay community as if it is uniform or easily identifiable. As with all communities, there is diversity in terms of how individuals wish to define themselves and live their lives.

The images which the popular media most perpetuate about gay men and lesbians are the stereotypes of either the effeminate, white, meticulously groomed and dressed, middle- to upper-class, urban man living in a fabulously decorated house or flat, or the butch, short-haired, motorcycle-riding woman wearing no jewellery or make up, who carries her wallet in her back pocket. Being gay or lesbian has also perhaps been viewed in some quarters as being only a "white thing".

But the reality is that, although some may fit those stereotypes, gay men and lesbians are as diverse as any other section of the general population, and they are part of every ethnic group, culture, religious and socio-economic affiliation and most families in Britain today.

Lesbians and gay men are frequently socialised to hide their sexual orientation, and therefore most form part of an invisible population. A search of the 2001 UK Census data yielded no results using the terms lesbian, gay, or homosexual, so it is not possible to document accurately the size of the gay and lesbian population. It is estimated, however, that between three and five per cent of the British population identify as lesbian or gay. In addition, in many areas of Britain (mostly outside of urban areas), it is still relatively unsafe for most lesbian or gay people to live openly and acknowledge their sexual orientation.

Terminology

Language is often a source of confusion and misinformation and, as such, it is important that service providers have accurate definitions. Heterosexual care providers are often unfamiliar or uncomfortable with the vernacular of the gay and lesbian culture. It should be recognised that, as with any sub-culture – particularly that of oppressed groups – language is constantly changing. Usage may vary with different generations, area of the country, socioeconomic status or cultural background. Which terms are acceptable and which are offensive varies widely and are also culturally dependent.

The use of the word homosexual in describing individuals and same-sex relationships may also be inaccurate. When referring to people, as opposed to behaviour, "homosexual" is considered derogatory and places emphasis on sex. The preferred terms are "gay" and "lesbian", which stress cultural and social matters over sex and sexual relationships.

In order that adoption and fostering social workers are clear about terminology and language, we describe below terms that relate to lesbians and gay men, to sex, gender and sexuality.

Sex, gender and sexuality

The English noun "**gender**" is derived from the Old French word *genre*, meaning "kind of thing". It goes back to the Latin word *genus* (meaning "kind", "species"). Gender is often, but decreasingly, used as a synonym for "sex", which refers to the physical anatomical differences that are commonly used to differentiate male from female.

Many people, among them social scientists, use **sex** to refer to the biological division into male and female, and **gender** to refer to gender roles assigned to people on the basis of their apparent sex and/or other associated factors. Society tends to assign some social roles to males and others to females (as society perceives their sex).

A person's gender is usually assigned at birth. The "boy" or "girl" recorded on the birth certificate can affect much of what happens to that child, socially, for the rest of their lives. Gender is a social, cultural, psychological and historical construct. It is used to describe people and their roles in society, the way they dress and how they are meant to behave.

It is assumed by some that **sex**, **gender** and **sexuality** naturally follow on from each other, but throughout different societies and cultures there have been very different notions of sex, gender and sexuality and how these are expressed. It is perhaps more helpful to consider the question: what is sexuality and how do people in different places and at different times understand their bodies and desires? **Sexuality** is usually defined as the expression of sexual desire.

Sexual orientation

This is the commonly accepted term for the direction of a person's sexual, emotional and/or physical attraction, and its expression. Examples of sexual orientation are **heterosexuality**, **homosexuality** and **bisexuality**. In a sense, sexual orientation is a social construct, and a relatively new one, most likely determined by a combination of continually interacting socio-cultural influences and biological tendencies. Most cultures have a sexual object preference for the opposite sex.

For many years the common assumption, shared by many scientists and religious communities, was that the natural and normal human sexual orientation is exclusively for the opposite sex (i.e. heterosexual). In 1976 the historian Michel Foucault argued that homosexuality as a concept did not exist as such in the 18th century; that people instead spoke of sodomy (which involved specific sexual acts, regardless of the sex or sexuality of the people involved). Studies carried out during and after the 1950s led psychologists and doctors to recognise homosexuality as a second exclusive orientation. Since then, similar acceptance has grown for non-exclusive orientations, such as bisexuality.

Heterosexuality
This term relates to sexual attraction, both physical and emotional, which is primarily directed toward persons of the opposite sex.

Homosexuality
This term relates to sexual attraction, both physical and emotional, which is primarily directed toward persons of the same sex.

The word *homosexual* translates literally as "of the same sex", being a hybrid of the Greek prefix *homo-* meaning "same" (as distinguished from the Latin root *homo* meaning human) and the Latin root *sex* meaning "sex". Although some early writers used the adjective homosexual to refer to any single-gender context (such as the Roman Catholic clergy or an all-girls' school), today the term implies a sexual aspect. The term *homosocial* is now used to describe single-sex contexts that are not specifically sexual. Older terms for homosexuality, such as *homophilia* and *inversion* (in which a gay individual would be called a "homophile" or an "invert") have fallen into disuse. The term homosexual can be used as a noun or adjective to describe same-sex oriented individuals as well as their sexual attractions and behaviours.

It is recommended by some that the terms homosexual and homosexuality be avoided. Describing individuals as homosexual may be offensive, partly because of the negative clinical association of the word stemming from its use in describing same-sex attraction as a pathological state before homosexuality was removed from lists of mental disorders. For example, the American Psychiatric Association's 1973 list of mental disorders still regarded homosexuality as confused or disturbed sexuality. In Britain in 1975, the *British Medical Journal* was still publishing articles on possible treatments for homosexuality, including hormonal therapy and aversion therapy. It was not until 1992 that the World Health Organisation deleted homosexuality from its list of mental disorders, with the UK government following suit in 1993.

Bisexuality
This term refers to sexual attraction towards people of both sexes. Someone who identifies as bisexual is attracted to, and may form sexual and affectionate relationships with, both men and women, though not necessarily at the same time. The term may refer to a socio-political identity or to sexual behaviour, or both. There have been people in most known societies who have exhibited some degree of bisexuality.

Although bisexuality is an identified sexual orientation, it is sometimes transitional for those coming to terms with their lesbian or gay identity. Some people identify as bisexual before identifying as gay or lesbian, because bisexuality can represent a mediating position between homosexual and heterosexual in the traditional cultural system.

Gay

In addition to meaning "merry", "joyous", or "glad", gay also means homosexual. Gay also refers to homosexually-oriented ideas (e.g. literature or values).

The word gay has had a sexual meaning since at least the nineteenth century (and possibly earlier). In Victorian England, female and male prostitutes were called "gay" because they dressed gaily. Eventually, "gay boys" (renters) became used as a term for any male homosexual. It has also been claimed that "gay" was an acronym for "Good As You"; another popular etymology places its origin in Gay Street, in New York's West Village, a local point of homosexual culture.

Gay can be used to refer only to male homosexuals. Used inclusively it refers to homosexual men and women, and arguably to bisexuals. When used in the phrase "the gay community" it may also include transgendered and transsexuals, although this is also a subject of some debate.

Gay originally was used purely as an adjective ('He is a gay man' or 'He is gay'). Gay is now also used as a collective noun (e.g.'Gays are opposed to that policy'), but rarely as a singular noun ('He is a gay'). When used as an adjective not describing a person who is part of the gay community (e.g. 'That hat is so gay'), the term 'gay' is purely pejorative and deeply offensive. The derogatory implication is that the object (or person) in question is inferior, weak, effeminate, or just stupid.

Lesbian

A lesbian is a woman whose homosexual orientation is self-defined, affirmed, or acknowledged as such. Lesbian also refers to female homosexually-oriented (and can refer to women-oriented) ideas, communities or varieties of cultural expression.

The word "lesbian" originally referred to an inhabitant of the Greek island of Lesbos. It came to have its current meaning because of the ancient Greek poet, Sappho, who lived on Lesbos; some of her poems concerned love between women. Whether Sappho was a lesbian, in the modern meaning of the term, or simply a poet who described lesbians, is open to question. Nevertheless, this association with Sappho led to the term "sapphism" being used as another term for lesbianism.

Transsexuals

These are people who desire to have, or have achieved, a different physical sex from that which they were assigned at birth. One typical (though oversimplified) explanation is of a "woman trapped in a man's body" or vice versa. Many transsexual women state that they were in fact always of the female gender, but were assigned the male gender as a child on the basis of their genitals, and having realised that they are female, wish to change their bodies to match; for transsexual men, the feeling is exactly the opposite. People whose gender identity is in conflict with their birth gender usually want to achieve a congruence of identity, role and anatomy by having sexual reassignment surgery. Most transsexuals identify as heterosexual.

Transgender

This is often used as a euphemistic synonym for transsexual people. One reason for this is that it removes the conceptual image "sex" from the term "transsexual" that implies that transsexuality is sexually motivated, which it is not. Transgender is also used to describe behaviour or feelings that cannot be categorised into other defined categories, for example, people living in a gender role that is different from the one they were assigned at birth, but who do not wish to undergo any or all of the available medical options, or people who do not wish to identify themselves as transsexuals, men or women, and consider that they fall between genders, or transcend gender. Many transsexuals reject the term "transgender" as an identification for themselves – either as a synonym or umbrella term. They argue that the term inaccurately subsumes them and therefore causes their identity, history and existence to be marginalised.

Transvestite/Cross-dresser

This is a person who, for any reason, wears the clothing of a gender other than that to which they were assigned at birth. Cross-dressers may have no desire or intention of adopting the behaviours or practices common to those of the other gender, and do not necessarily wish to undergo medical procedures to facilitate physical changes. Contrary to common belief, most male-bodied cross-dressers prefer female partners.

Bull dyke, fag and queer

These terms are sometimes used to refer negatively to lesbians and gay men. They are equivalent to hate terms and epithets used against some minority ethnic groups. There is a political usage for words such as queer, dyke or faggot by some gays and lesbians who, in a reclamation process, redefine and use with pride words formerly used pejoratively. However, because these words still carry a negative connotation in society, their positive usage is restricted to political lesbians and gay men active in the reclamation struggle.

Drag

The term "drag queen" originates in *Polari*, the language of gay men in England in the early part of the last century. "Drag" meant "clothes", and was also theatre slang for a woman's costume worn by a male actor. A "queen" is an effeminate gay man. Drag is a part of Western gay culture – drag involves wearing highly exaggerated and outrageous costumes or imitating movie and music stars of the opposite sex. It is a form of performing art practised by drag queens and kings. Female-bodied people who perform in usually exaggerated men's clothes and personae are called "drag kings", although this term has a wider meaning than drag queen.

Heterosexism (or heterocentrism or heterosexualism)

This is the assumption that everyone or a particular person is heterosexual. It does not necessarily imply hostility towards other sexual orientations (as does homophobia), but is merely a failure to recognise their existence. Heterocentrism is culturally, religiously and socially sanctioned by most major institutions in British culture, including the family.

Homophobia

This term is most frequently used to describe any sort of opposition to homosexual behaviour or the political causes associated with homosexuality, although this opposition may more accurately be called "anti-gay bias".

The term also describes a phobia triggered by an encounter (in self or others) with same-sex physical attraction, love and sexuality. Described by George Weinberg (1973), the clinical psychologist who coined the term, as a morbid and irrational fear, homophobia can express itself as hatred of or aversion to homosexual feelings and behaviours, and of the people perceived as exhibiting them. Such feelings can result in aggressive behaviour directed against the person or situation triggering the phobia.

Homo-ignorant

A term developed to describe individuals with a very limited knowledge about gays, lesbians, bisexual, and transgender individuals.

Coming out

Coming out (see Coleman 1981; Cass 1979, 1984; Troiden 1979, 1993) is defined as, 'The developmental process through which gay and lesbian people recognise their sexual orientation and integrate this knowledge into their personal and social lives' (De Monteflores and Schultz, 1978, p.59). Coming out is the process of first recognising and then acknowledging non-heterosexual orientation to oneself, and then disclosing it to others. Coming out often occurs in stages and is a non-linear process. Coming out can also be used to mean "disclosure", as in 'I just came out to my parents'.

Disclosure

Disclosure is the point at which a lesbian or gay man discloses their sexual orientation to another person. It is not appropriate to use terms such as discovered, admitted, revealed, found out, declared, which are pejorative terms, suggesting judgement.

Being out

This term is used to describe a person who is open about their sexual orientation to friends, family, colleagues, and society. Not everyone who is "out" is "out" to all of these groups; some people may be out to their family, but not to their colleagues.

Being closeted or in the closet

These terms refer to someone who is not open about her/his sexual orientation. This person, for their own reasons, chooses to hide their sexual orientation from others.

Common questions and presumptions

This section deals with some of the myths and questions that social workers, in our experience, have about lesbians and gay men. In the absence of accurate information, many professionals rely on their own knowledge, which may be shaped by stereotypes and myths. We are brought up in a society that presumes heterosexuality as the norm, and this is expressed through language and behaviour, which in turn are often based in myths and stereotypes. Here are some common questions and presumptions.

How do you know if a person is lesbian or gay?

For the most part, knowing whether or not a person is gay or lesbian is all about paying attention to feelings of attraction. It is very difficult for many people to be honest with themselves about same-gender attraction because society is, in general, unaccepting of lesbians and gay men.

While some young people believe they are gay or lesbian in their adolescence, others do not have or acknowledge these feelings until much later. Coming out is a process which can occur at any time in life.

Can someone be lesbian or gay without ever having had a homosexual experience or relationship?

Yes. Some lesbians and gay men have never had a sexual relationship with another person, yet know they are lesbian or gay. Sexual orientation has more to do with internal feelings – one's sense of "affectional fit", rather than actual sexual experience.

Can someone have homosexual feelings and not be lesbian or gay? Can someone have heterosexual feelings and not be a heterosexual?

Yes. Human sexuality is very complex and not easily separated into rigid categories. It is perfectly natural for a gay man or lesbian to have feelings of attraction for someone of the opposite gender, just as it is perfectly natural for a heterosexual person to have feelings of attraction for a person of the same gender. Although almost everyone experiences these feelings at one time or another, they can be confusing. Many people struggling with issues of sexual orientation will test out their feelings with both males and females. It is important to remember that people will eventually "be who they are". Nothing that anyone tells them or says to encourage or dissuade them will change their sexual orientation. Sexuality and sexual/gender identity are a very complex area of practice, and social workers must develop skills for dealing with the ambiguity of sexual identity.

If you have had a same-sex sexual experience, does that make you gay or lesbian?

Not necessarily, because being lesbian or gay is not just about sexual behaviour. The sexual aspect of a lesbian or gay person's life is, of course, important, but to focus exclusively on those aspects is a mistake. Knowing that you are lesbian or gay is more than just sexual behaviour.

Social workers need to be clear for themselves and for the users with whom they work, that sexual orientation and sexuality involve many aspects of identity and relationship that go beyond sexual behaviour. The "Sexuality Flower" by Jo Adams and Carol Painter (Centre for HIV and Sexual Health, SE Sheffield Primary Care Trust)* represents a holistic approach to sexuality and illustrates that everyone

has a sexuality, even if they are celibate. Like all flowers, aspects of our sexuality need nurturing.

How many lesbians and gay men are there?

Although there has been a great deal of discussion about the size of the lesbian and gay population, the reality is that since it is still stigmatising for some people to identify as such, many lesbians and gay men hide their sexuality. It is therefore very difficult to ascertain how many lesbians and gay men there are.

Have there always been lesbians and gay men?

Yes. There is evidence of the existence of homosexuality throughout history, as depicted in art, literature and music. Famous lesbians and gay men throughout history include: Plato, Alexander the Great, Leonardo Da Vinci, Michelangelo, James I, Tchaikovsky, Oscar Wilde, award-winning British actor Sir Ian McKellen, Virginia Woolf, Noel Coward, Cole Porter, poet Niki Giovanni, British economist and Nobel Prize winner John Maynard Keynes, songwriter Billy Strayhorn, Spanish filmmaker Pedro Almodovar, Jamaican writer Michelle Cliff, British writer Christopher Isherwood, poet/writer Audre Lorde, British mathematician and computer scientist Alan Turing, British writer Vita Sackville-West, actor Miriam Margoyles, writer James Baldwin, poet Langston Hughes, singer Melissa Etheridge, African-American chaplain of Harvard University Rev Peter Gomes, and tennis champion Martina Navratilova.

How do you become lesbian or gay?

You cannot *become* lesbian or gay, any more than a person *becomes* heterosexual. Since sexual identity emanates from an internal sense of fit, most lesbians and gay men become aware of these feelings as they grow. Exactly where these feelings come from and why remains an unknown factor.

Are some people born lesbian or gay?

There is preliminary research evidence (LeVay, 1994) that strongly suggests a genetic and biological basis for sexual orientation. Although many gay males, some bisexuals, some transgender people and some lesbians recall that they have always known that they were "different", others do not agree with the "gay from birth" philosophy. The research in this area is very limited.

Is being lesbian or gay a choice for some people?

Just as heterosexual people do not choose their sexual orientation, the large majority of lesbians and gay

* More details about the "Sexuality Flower" and about *Explore Dream Discover*, an information pack based around this idea, can be requested from Rachel Hunt on 0114 226 1912, or email rachel.hunt@chiv.nhs.uk.

men do not choose theirs. The only real choice that most lesbians and gay men have to deal with is whether or not to be open about their orientation. Some lesbians and gay men, however, do envision their entire identity as a social construction – a series of choices that one makes about their lives. These individuals feel that it is their choice, not society's, to determine how and what to do.

Can someone be seduced into being lesbian or gay?

No, it is simply not possible for someone to be seduced into being gay, any more than a gay man or a lesbian could be seduced into being heterosexual.

Are lesbians or gay men more likely to abuse a child?

No. The most likely person to abuse a child, according to researchers, is a heterosexual male who is known to the child's family (Jenny *et al*, 1994). But despite this clear evidence, the terms "gay" and "child sexual abuser" are very often wrongly used synonymously by some.

Does the experience of being sexually abused as a child make you lesbian or gay?

Although some lesbians and gay men were sexually abused as children, just as some heterosexual men and women were, there is no evidence to suggest that being sexually abused makes someone gay or lesbian.

Are lesbians and gay men the way they are because they have not met the right man or woman?

No. In fact, many gay men and lesbians have been married or have had partners of the opposite sex. Being lesbian or gay is not a matter of meeting the right person of the opposite sex again; it is about finding the right internal sense of fit with a person, which usually is a person of the same sex.

Couldn't lesbians and gay men really be heterosexual if they tried?

Many lesbians and gay men have tried to be heterosexual. Being lesbian or gay is so condemned by some in society that many lesbians and gay men try to pretend to be heterosexual, at least for part of their lives. Some try for a lifetime, never acting on or acknowledging their true feelings, some find ways to adapt to their feelings through furtive relationships, and others remain married for years.

How can you tell if a person is lesbian or gay?

Although at one time many people thought that lesbians and gay men were identifiable through stereotypical mannerisms, affectations, dress and so on, the only real way to tell if someone is lesbian or gay is if they tell you. Too often social workers continue to look for the stereotypical, non-conforming behaviours or mannerisms, but by and large, lesbians and gay men are a very diverse group from different ethnic backgrounds, cultures and religions, and of different ages, temperaments, and degrees of masculinity and femininity.

Are lesbians and gay men normal?

If normal means the majority, then gay and lesbian persons aren't normal by this definition. If you are left-handed you are not in the majority, and yet you would be viewed as normal. Most lesbians and gay men believe that their sexual orientation is a normal variation on the wide spectrum of sexual orientation.

Is there a lesbian or gay culture?

There are lesbians and gay men of all cultures, ethnic backgrounds, religions and social classes. In as much as lesbians and gay men adopt the norms of their particular cultures, lesbians and gay men also have their own language, humour, styles of dress, social events and norms. Lesbian and gay culture is diverse, so it is important for workers to listen carefully to the individuals they are working with, and understand what being lesbian or gay means for them.

Is there a lesbian or gay lifestyle?

Most lesbians and gay men object to this term because it trivialises lesbian and gay men's lives. If you are a lesbian or gay man then you have a life, not a lifestyle. Just as there is no such thing as a heterosexual lifestyle, there is no such thing as a lesbian or gay lifestyle.

Do gay men dislike women, and do lesbians dislike men?

There are often tensions between men and women. Some gay men dislike women and some lesbians dislike men, just like some heterosexual men dislike women and some heterosexual women dislike men. But, in general, gay men do not dislike women and lesbians do not dislike men.

Do gay men and lesbians dislike heterosexual people?

Some lesbian and gay people have hostile feelings towards heterosexuals, but generally, the answer to this question is no. Lesbians and gay men have experienced discrimination and prejudice at the hands of heterosexuals, but all have heterosexuals amongst their family and friends.

Why do so many people have trouble accepting lesbians and gay men?

Discussion of sex and sexuality makes many people feel uncomfortable. Homosexuality, in particular, appears to generate strong feelings in some people. Many people have difficulty accepting lesbians and gay men because of their own religious beliefs or moral perspectives. Some people are uncomfortable dealing with lesbians and gay men because of their own biases. It is important to begin to understand the nature of homophobia that exists in society, and as part of this to be willing to engage in examining our own attitudes and values in relation to sexual orientations that are different to our own.

Coming out and self-identity

From a practice perspective, it is essential that family placement social workers acknowledge that coming out is a process which can happen at any stage in an individual's life.

Gay men and lesbians may be out in some situations or to certain family members or associates, and not others, e.g. some may be out only to lesbian or gay friends, others to friends who are not lesbian or gay. Still others who self-identify as lesbian or gay are out to everyone – families, friends, employers, co-workers and the wider community. Some people may never come out to anyone besides themselves. It is, in fact, possible for someone never to admit their sexual orientation even to themselves, although there can be great psychological consequences for not doing so.

Coming out is a very personal and unique situation for each individual; homophobia is still so prevalent in society that many lesbians and gay men choose to stay closeted for many different reasons. Black and/or disabled lesbians and gay men may live with the dual tensions associated with coming out and, as such, may opt to stay closeted to avoid further pressures.

Coming out as a lesbian or gay man during adolescence may be a very different experience than coming out as an adult. Consequently, some people move through the process smoothly, accepting their sexual orientation, making social contacts, and finding a good fit within their environments. Others are unnerved by their sexual orientation, vacillating in their conviction, hiding in their uneasiness, and struggling to find their place. In addition, there are different levels of "outness" or "openness" about one's sexual orientation.

"Race" and ethnicity can also affect the coming out process. Black people, many of whom have experienced significant stress related to oppression and racism based on skin colour or ethnicity, may experience even greater difficulty coming out, especially within the family context (Greene, 1994; Savin-Williams and Rodriguez, 1993; Walters 1998). There have been many black lesbians and gay men throughout history, some of them have already been mentioned earlier. There are in the UK a number of supportive networks and groups for black lesbians and gay men, organised along racial/religious lines, e.g. Imaan and KISS.

Individuals within the black communities who identify themselves as lesbian or gay may become aware of their difference in adolescence and must not only deal with the stigma within their own cultural/racial community but must also find a supportive lesbian/gay community to which they can relate. The lesbian/gay community is often a microcosm of society, and many black gay men and lesbians confront racism in it. To sustain oneself in three distinct communities requires an enormous effort and can also produce stress for both the adolescent and adult (Hunter and Schaecher, 1987; Morales, 1989).

Internalised homophobia

When I first came out, at 25, I was really turned off by effeminate gay men. Drag queens really made me crazy. I didn't want anyone thinking that I was like that. After a while, I realized how homophobic that kind of thinking was. I mean, what did I think – I was better than them because I was butch? In reality, whether I wanted people to see me as masculine or not, some people in society would always think of gay men as "fairies" and there wasn't anything I could do to change that. I guess, it took me a while to get comfortable about my gay identity and to realize that as gay people we are a very diverse group, which includes drag queens and butch men.

Some psychological research suggests that "internalised homophobia" is a normal part of the process of coming out (Forstein, 1988; Maylon, 1982; Shidlo, 1994). Lesbians and gay men grow up in a heterosexual world that continually tells them they are wrong. They are taught to believe that heterosexuality is the only option and that homosexuality is a perversion. Thus, many young lesbians and gay men fall victim to Shidlo's (1994) definition of internalised homophobia: 'A set of negative attitudes and affects toward homosexuality in other persons and toward homosexual features in oneself' (p.178). These feelings can significantly impede the self-acceptance process that many gay men and lesbians must go through in order to come out.

Psychology researchers Fassinger and Miller explain that there are two models of identity development for gay men and lesbians: 1) an individual development of sexual identity that includes acceptance of a lesbian or gay orientation, and 2) the development of a group membership identity, involving the acceptance of membership in an oppressed group and developing affiliations within that group (Fassinger and Miller, cited in Mayfield, 2001, p.55). Thus an individual could accept themselves but not be accepting of the lesbian or gay community in general. Negative attitudes towards lesbian and gay culture may be seen as an alternative type of internalised homophobia.

Internalised homophobia is rooted in the shame our society places on homosexuality. Overcoming that shame in oneself is the first step towards self-acceptance and, in turn, acceptance of the lesbian and gay community.

Conclusion

This chapter summarises the images and demography of the lesbian and gay population in the UK. Commonly-used terms and professional terminology are defined for social workers who are working with or intend to work with lesbians and gay men. In addition, myths and stereotypes about lesbians and gay men, frequently used in the absence of accurate information, are identified and dispelled. Some common questions and presumptions about gay men and lesbians are illuminated for the reader. Finally, the process of coming out and a discussion of lesbian and gay identity are discussed and highlighted for the social work practitioner.

3 The legal context

The political debate that has taken place over the past four decades has highlighted the level of homophobia that permeates our society. It is worth noting that it was not until December 2003 that discrimination at work on the grounds of sexual orientation was made illegal in the UK.

Discrimination against gay men and lesbians in Britain has been reflected in legislation and policy over the past forty years. This chapter provides an overview of the changes in UK law* and policy relating to lesbians and gay men in two particular areas of life:

- their sexual practices;

- their freedom and right to be parents.

There have been positive changes in the last ten years, in terms of a political shift in attitudes, which are reflected in legislation. However, the day-to-day realities of life for many lesbians and gay men have not been affected by these shifts – particularly in the areas of family life and parenting. Legislation and policy have been shaped by, and in turn have influenced, attitudes towards gay and lesbian relationships and parenting, and have also influenced decision-making in terms of what is in the best interests of children in terms of family life.

The criminalisation of gay sex

Over the last hundred years, there have been a number of legislative measures that have focused on the sexual practices of gay men.** This has served to equate the expression of sexuality with sex, and in particular has influenced attitudes towards gay men in terms of the nature of their relationships and suitability to be parents.

Victorian legislation

Two Victorian scandals shaped Britain's sex law, the Criminal Law (Amendment) Act 1885, which

remained in place for a century. The first scandal was triggered in July 1885 when the crusading journalist WT Stead revealed the "white slave" traffic at the heart of the British Empire. He was jailed for showing it was possible in London to buy a 13-year-old girl for sex. The scandal led to legislation raising the age of consent for sex from 13 to 16 for girls. But the Criminal Law Amendment Bill was ambushed by Henry Labouchere, a republican Liberal MP, who proposed it should also make any form of sex between men a crime. Anal sex had been illegal since the reign of Henry VIII but the Labouchere amendment extended punishment to 'any act of gross indecency'. There was little debate, and the Bill became law in August 1885. The main concern was that it might become a 'blackmailer's charter'.

Section II of the Act provided for a term of imprisonment not exceeding two years, with or without hard labour, for any male person guilty of an act of gross indecency with another male person in public or in private. This unleashed a wave of homophobic witch-hunts, which began with the sensational Cleveland Street scandal of 1889. It was revealed that two peers of the realm, Lord Arthur Somerset and Lord Euston, and, it was claimed, Prince Eddy, the son of the Prince of Wales, had visited a male brothel in London where Post Office telegram delivery boys were "corrupted" for four shillings a time. The scandal cemented public support for the legislation. The trial and imprisonment of Oscar Wilde for gross indecency followed in 1895 amid an intense newspaper campaign against 'the buggers'.

Twentieth-century legislation

The Sexual Offences Act of 1956 was a consolidation of the original Victorian statute of 1885 and was passed in three minutes without real debate. Offences of buggery and gross indecency between men were offences under sections 12 and 13 of the Act, which criminalised consensual homosexual activity.

---

* There are variations in legislation in different parts of the UK.
** The legislation did not criminalise lesbianism. Hansard records that when one peer tried to raise the issue he was told to "shut up", on the grounds that he would only advertise its existence to an impressionable public. Legend has it that Queen Victoria believed that sexual activity between women did not exist, therefore there has been no equivalent legislation in relation to lesbian sexual activity.

The Sexual Offences Act 1967 legalised consensual adult homosexual activity for men over 21 with the stipulation that it occur only in private and with no more than two people present. It was 1980 before this happened in Scotland, 1982 in Northern Ireland and 1992 in the Isle of Man.

The Sexual Offences Bill 2003 received Royal Assent in November of that year. The offences of buggery and indecency between men were repealed. Men who have been convicted of these offences where the activity was consensual and the victim was over 16 will be taken off the sex offenders register. The "privacy" provision, which outlaws gay sex involving more than one person (Section 1 of the Sexual Offences Act 1967), was also repealed. The new Act introduced a new offence, outlawing straight or gay sex acts in any public place, where participants know that people who are not willing observers may be able to see them.

Up until January 2000, gay men and lesbians were barred from entering the armed forces, and had to keep their sexual orientation hidden. This changed after two legal cases in 1998, when two members of the forces threatened with dismissal because of their sexual orientation took their case to the High Court, and then to the European Court of Human Rights. Their cases were supported by Stonewall, the lobbying group for lesbians, gay men and bisexuals. After the cases were won, the government acted to lift the ban. Today, lesbians and gay men in the armed forces can expect to receive treatment equal to that of any other member.

Age of consent

In 1994 the House of Commons voted to reduce the gay male age of consent to 18. Although there was a push for equalising the age of consent at this time with that for heterosexual people, 18 was accepted as a compromise under the guise that males developed more slowly than females.

In May 1996 the European Court of Human Rights (ECHR) agreed to hear the case of Euan Sutherland, which challenged the unequal age of consent. On 7 October 1997, the ECHR ruled that the unequal age of consent was unlawful, prompting the government to grant a free vote in the Commons regarding the matter. In June 1998, the House of Commons voted 336 – 129 to equalise the age of consent. In July, the House of Lords rejected 290 – 122 the amendment to the Crime and Disorder Bill 1998 which would have equalised the age of consent at 16.

In January 1999, there was a further vote in the Commons, 313 – 130, to equalise the age of consent, this time as part of the Sexual Offences Bill 1999. The Lords again threw out the Commons vote, meaning that the age of consent for gay males remained at 18. In November 2000, the Parliament Act was invoked and its provisions ensured that the Sexual Offences (Amendment) Bill was passed for Royal Assent, lowering the age of consent to 16, in line with heterosexuals; in Northern Ireland it is 17.

The public and parliamentary debate relating to the age of consent again demonstrates some of the homophobic attitudes that are ingrained and pervasive in some sectors of society. An equal age of consent and the decriminalisation of gay sex have begun to address the inequality and discrimination faced by many gay men in this area of their lives.

Family life and parenting

Almost two decades ago, Helen Cosis-Brown (1998) forewarned:

> *The perceived threat of lesbian and gay households parenting children, to children, the family and society, has been a powerful force over a considerable period. (p.90)*

This prediction was reflected in two newspapers in 2004:

> *Britain has experienced an explosion in gay adoption since it became legal a year ago... as a result, heterosexual couples are facing even greater obstacles than they have in the past – including, in some areas, being banned if they themselves disapprove of gay adoptions. (Daily Mail, January 2004)*

A front page article in *The Daily Express* in October 2004 questions how gay dads could be "allowed" to adopt three little children, and quotes Ann Widdecombe as saying,

> *It is making a mockery of the law. My view is that we should always look to place children for adoption with mothers and fathers who are married and have been in a long-term relationship.*

Helen Cosis-Brown (1998) observed that it is likely that lesbians and gay men have always cared for other people's children, but 'it is the public acknowledgement of this that has appeared to be intolerable'.

England and Wales

The debates generated by the guidance and regulations relating to fostering with the introduction of the Children Act 1989 and the Adoption White Paper in the early 1990s are testament to this sentiment.

> It would be wrong to arbitrarily exclude any particular groups of people from consideration, but the chosen way of life of some adults may mean that they are not able to provide a suitable environment for the care and nurture of a child. No one has the 'right' to be a foster parent. Fostering decisions must centre exclusively on the interests of the child. (Department of Health, 1991)

Paragraph 16 of the consultation paper (Department of Health (DH), 1990) originally stated that 'equal rights' and 'gay rights' policies have no place in fostering services. The reference to gay rights was removed from the published guidance (DH, 1991) as a result of protest and debate. The reference to a 'chosen way of life' remained, and as Hicks and McDermott (1999, p.195) observe, this 'effectively reduces the complexity of lesbian and gay experience, identity and politics to a "lifestyle choice" and this is open to discriminatory interpretation with regard to sexuality'. The Positive Parenting Campaign was formed in Manchester specifically to challenge paragraph 16.

The same guidance (DH, 1991, para. 9.53) went on to state that the needs and concerns of young lesbians and gay men being fostered should also be acknowledged, recognised and approached sympathetically. 'Gay young men and women may require very sympathetic carers to enable them to accept their sexuality and to develop their own self-esteem' (DH, 1991, para. 98). However, the message from the government at this time was clear; it was not sympathetic to the recruitment and approval of lesbian and gay carers.

The review of adoption law in the early 1990s saw similar arguments being put forward. The Adoption Law Review Discussion Paper No 3 included a section on lesbians and gay male homosexuals. This reads:

> The question of adoption by lesbians or male homosexuals, whether living with a partner or not, is controversial. There is one view that such applicants should not be excluded from consideration if they can satisfy an agency that they can provide a home in which a child's interests would be safeguarded and promoted. Others take the view that placement with a lesbian or male homosexual could never be in a child's interests and could never provide a suitable environment for the care and nurture of a child. Views would be welcomed. (DH/Welsh Office, 1992a)

Views *were* forthcoming, and the government found itself at odds with professional opinion in both social work and childcare fields. The report to ministers in 1992 states:

> We do not propose any changes to the law relating to single applicants, including lesbians and gay men. There are examples of extremely successful adoptions, particularly of older children and children with disabilities, by single adopters. (DH/Welsh Office, 1992b, para. 50)

Tim Yeo, Health Minister at the time, insisted that 'the vast majority of children benefit from having two loving parents of opposite sexes, and adoption agencies should make strenuous efforts to find such couples' (reported in Marchant, 1992, p.1). Lesbian and gay applicants were viewed, therefore, as Hicks (1996) had earlier put it, as a 'last resort'.

The White Paper *Adoption: The future* (DH, 1993) barely mentions lesbians and gay men. It emphasises that adoption by married couples should be the preferred option other than in 'exceptional circumstances'. In effect, the White Paper set up a hierarchy of acceptable family structures. It suggested that 'common sense' should prevail in decisions about assessing prospective adopters. It confirmed the unofficial policy of some agencies making placements of disabled or traditionally "hard-to-place" children with lesbians and gay men. Put bluntly – second best adopters for last choice children.

In 1994, The Children's Society barred lesbian and gay applicants from applying to foster or adopt. The ban aimed to ensure that the Society's procedures remained in line with its avowed Christian principles. It was five years before the ban was lifted in 1999 and was very controversial, with some funders even withdrawing their support.

In March 1996, a draft Adoption Bill was published, but failed to make an appearance in John Major's last parliamentary session as Prime Minister. The advent of a Labour government led to expectations of legislation, and in 2000 Prime Minister Tony Blair announced his review of adoption, which was completed by July of that year. The review was followed by the White Paper, *Adoption: A new approach*, accompanied by new National Adoption Standards. The draft Adoption Bill was published in March 2001.

In the meantime, developments in case law were challenging the notion that lesbians and gay men were unsuitable as foster and adoptive parents. In 1994, *Re C*, a joint residence order was granted to a lesbian (who had a child by artificial insemination) and her partner, giving both partners parental responsibility in law (Beresford, 1994). This is not, however, an *equal* sharing of responsibility – see discussion below. A court judgment in 1997, *Re W (a minor) (Adoption a homosexual adopter)*, found nothing in current adoption law to preclude a single person applying to adopt, even if they were living in a lesbian or gay relationship at the time, and that any other decision to prevent this on the grounds of sexual orientation would be 'illogical, arbitrary and inappropriately discriminatory' (*The Times*, 21 May 1997). The Scottish courts had previously reached similar conclusions in *T, Petitioner 1997* (SLT. 724. Reported in *Adoption & Fostering*, 20:3, 1996, p.47).

In November 2002, the Adoption and Children Act 2002 received Royal Assent, giving unmarried and same-sex couples the right to adopt jointly. Such couples would need to be able to demonstrate that their partnership is stable and permanent (Suitability of Adopters Regulations 2005). From the time of full implementation of the new Act – planned for 30 December 2005 – unmarried and same-sex couples will be able to adopt jointly. Further legal consequences of the Adoption and Children Act 2002 for same-sex couples are discussed below.

There was wide-ranging debate between 2000 and 2002 during the process of reform about whether families other than those headed by married couples should be approved as prospective adopters. The idea that single or unmarried parenthood was a last resort echoes some of the views expressed ten years earlier when the White Paper *Adoption: The future* was debated: 'The alternative to adoption, in the case of a child who has been in care, is so infinitely worse than adoption into a home which is less than ideal, that I believe the risk is justified' (Lady Saltoun of Abernathy – reported in Hansard, 11.7.2002, column CWH232). The Prime Minister's *Review of Adoption* (PIU, 2000) concluded that: '(study evidence) does not suggest that there are any over-riding factors which should exclude any particular group of people' (p.40).

It is worth noting that a well organised and well-funded Christian right-wing campaign was influential throughout the debate on the draft Adoption and Children Bill. The Christian Institute sent copies of Patricia Morgan's book *Children as Trophies?* (2002) to all MPs, fostering and adoption agencies, and panel medical advisers across the UK. The book claims to be an objective examination of evidence of same-sex parenting. The title comes from a quote from Jack Straw speaking on the Radio 4 Today programme on 4 November 1998:

> *I'm not in favour of gay couples seeking to adopt children because I question whether that is the right start in life. We should not see children as trophies. Children, in my judgment, and I think it is the judgment of almost everyone, including single parents, are best brought up where you have two natural parents in a stable relationship. There's no question about that. What we know from the evidence is that, generally speaking, stability is more likely to occur where the parents are married than when they are not.*

Morgan puts forward many arguments in her book as to why lesbians and gay men do not make suitable parents for the 'most vulnerable of children, often having endured all manner of deprivation, disruptions and disturbances' (p.130). For example, she argues that the 'lifespan of homosexuals is on average so much shorter than heterosexuals' (p.130). She goes on to assert that adoption agencies 'relatively unfavoured' other categories of people with short lifespans, such as smokers, older people and those with serious medical conditions – as 'particularly vulnerable children are more likely to be orphaned, or orphaned at a younger age'. Morgan's evidence that homosexuals have a shortened lifespan is based on a Canadian study of young gay and bisexual men with HIV infection. The life expectancy at the age of 20 for this group is 8–20 years less than for all men. How the evidence from this study is relevant to lesbians and gay men who do not have HIV infection is not immediately obvious. Morgan concludes:

> *Moreover, from the perspective of the "best interests of the child", if homosexual activity – like intravenous drug use – is lifeshortening, and morbidity attracting, then children should be placed with parents who, at the very least, will not steer them towards this. Homosexual parents seem considerably more likely to raise homosexual children. If people are making judgments about where to place children, then*

is it possible to ignore the differences between ways of life? (p.132)

Scotland

A review of adoption policy in Scotland has very recently completed its second phase, and the working group has reported back to ministers and recommended that unmarried couples, including same-sex couples, be allowed to adopt jointly. Under the first major change to adoption law in over 25 years, the law will, amongst other things, allow unmarried couples, including same-sex couples who are in enduring family relationships, to adopt jointly. Unmarried couples can, to all intents and purposes, adopt at present – both partners are assessed together but only one can apply to adopt while the other must apply for a residence order. In June 2005, the Scottish Executive announced:

> *This confusing legal position needs to be addressed. The Executive supports the group's unanimous recommendation, set within the context of decisions being made in the best interests of the child.* (Deputy Education Minister Euan Robson, BAAF Scottish Legal Group conference, Dundee, June 2005)

However, the fostering of children by same-sex couples is specifically prohibited under the Fostering of Children (Scotland) Regulations 1996. In all circumstances, if a single person applies to be a foster carer, any other adult living in the household must be related to that applicant, thereby precluding one member of a co-habiting same-sex couple, or even a single person who shares a house with others, from becoming a foster carer.

Northern Ireland

The Adoption (Northern Ireland) Order 1987 allows only single people or married couples to adopt; this means that only one partner from a lesbian or gay couple can be the adopter. There is no prohibition on lesbians and gay men fostering as single people or as partners. The first known reported case to consider the compatibility between a child's welfare interests and adoption by lesbian carers was *Re M (adoption: joint residence order: same sex couple)* in January 2004. All concerned looked to the 'sustained quality of care provided and unhesitatingly concluded that the welfare interests of this child would be best served by this couple'.

National Minimum Standards

Adoption and foster care agencies should have equal opportunities statements which acknowledge the requirement for them not to discriminate against potential applicants unlawfully. The National Minimum Standards for local authority adoption services in England and Wales (DH, 2003) state that 'Plans for recruitment will specify that people who are interested in becoming adoptive parents will be welcomed without prejudice... and (that they) will be treated fairly, openly and with respect throughout the adoption process' (Standard 3.1). The standards acknowledge that some voluntary agencies may have specific eligibility criteria, e.g. 'because it has particular religious beliefs... the prospective adopter is told what these are at the beginning of the process and, if necessary, is referred to another adoption agency' (Standard 14.4).

Human Rights Act

Article 14 of the Human Rights Act 1998 prohibits discrimination 'on any ground such as race, colour, language, religion, political or other opinion, national or social origin, association with a national minority, property, birth or other status'. A case heard before the ECHR in 2001, *Salgueiro da Silva Mouta v Portugal*, held that Article 8 of the European Convention on Human Rights had been breached by denying parental responsibility to a father on the grounds of his homosexuality. A commentary on this case notes that 'the English courts have now accepted that there is no general reason for believing that sexual orientation is a significant issue in itself'. (*Butterworths Family and Child Law Bulletin* 50, p.11)

Section 28

In tandem with the debate relating to lesbians and gay men as potential foster carers and adoptive parents in the late 1980s and early 1990s, another piece of legislation arrived on the statute books, introducing the notion of the "pretend" family. On 24 May 1988, Section 28 of the Local Government Act was enacted whereby a local authority could not 'intentionally promote homosexuality or publish material with the intention of promoting homosexuality' nor promote any 'teaching in maintained schools of the acceptability of homosexuality as a pretended family relationship'. This piece of legislation began its existence as a House of Lords initiative, a re-draft of a Private Members Bill introduced by Lord Halsbury in 1986. It was called an 'Act to refrain local authorities from promoting homosexuality'. It passed through the Lords, but fell in the Commons due to a lack of support.

The 1987 general election followed, and the political mood changed. In her campaigning speeches, Margaret Thatcher had announced her intention to make radical educational reforms, changing school syllabuses and returning to educational "basics". In her victory speech, Prime Minister Thatcher stated: 'Children who should be taught to respect traditional moral values, are being taught that they have an unalienable right to be gay'. Essentially, Section 28 allowed the Thatcher government to reassert "family values" at the expense of equal opportunities. Never before had homosexuality been discussed so much in public. When the Bill was introduced, Dame Jill Knight predicted there would be no need for legal action, given that self-censorship would have the desired effect of ending the services and profile of gay groups. Dame Jill was proved right: Section 28 was never tested in law – fear of prosecution kept it effective.

But there was opposition. In 1989, the campaigning group Stonewall was launched in response to Section 28. In July 2000, a move by the Labour government to repeal Section 28 was defeated in the House of Lords by 270 to 228 votes. It was not until July 2003 that the House of Lords finally voted to repeal Section 28.

Section 28 was repealed in Scotland in June 2000. In its consultation paper, the Scottish Executive stated:

This piece of legislation was, and remains, ill conceived. Its existence has served to legitimise intolerance and prejudice and, arguably, to raise the level of homophobia, acted as an unhelpful constraint on the ability of local authorities to develop best practice in sex education and bullying, and constrained the ability of local authorities to provide grants or funds to gay and lesbian groups in the community.

Civil partnership

Nine countries in the EU and some states in the USA and Australia already have some provision for recognising those in committed same-sex partnerships. On 18 November 2004, the Civil Partnership Bill was passed in the House of Lords by 251 votes to 136. At the third reading in the House of

Commons on 9 November 2004, MPs supported the Bill by 389 to 47.

The Civil Partnership Act 2004 comes into force on 5 December 2005, and civil registrations will be possible from 21 December 2005. This is a UK Act with separate provisions for England and Wales, for Northern Ireland and for Scotland.

The Act provides for legal recognition of same-sex partnerships. Couples will be able to enter civil partnerships in local registration services, and the register would have to be signed by each partner in the presence of two witnesses. There will also be a formal court-based process for dissolving the partnership. Civil registered partners will acquire the same legal rights and obligations as married couples. The main partnership rights included in the Act relate to social security and pension benefits, including the right to benefit from a dead partner's pension; full recognition of a partnership for the purposes of life assurance; an ability to succeed to tenancy rights; and next of kin visiting rights in hospital. In terms of responsibilities, the Act allows a partner with parental responsibility for a child (by birth or adoption) to agree to share parental responsibility with the other partner, or for the other partner to acquire parental responsibility by a court order (Section 4, Children Act 1989).

The Act will require extensive amendments to tax and benefit systems as well as training for registrars. Jacqui Smith MP said in 2003:

Same-sex couples often face a range of humiliating, distressing and unnecessary problems because of a lack of legal recognition. Civil partnership registration would underline the inherent value of committed same-sex relationships.

As noted previously, lesbians and gay men have always been involved in having and raising children (Hicks and McDermott, 1999, p.147). There is perhaps, now, greater acceptance in policy terms that lesbian and gay families are no longer "pretend families", and that these relationships are at the very least recognised in law, and that their "inherent value" will, over time, receive affirmation.

Unequal sharing of parental responsibility

Under current legislation in England and Wales, same-sex or unmarried heterosexual couples can only achieve a sharing of parental responsibility for an adoptive child by one partner obtaining an adoption order, and the other partner obtaining a residence order. This arrangement is not, however, an equal sharing of parental responsibility because the adoptive parent has complete and permanent parental responsibility – becoming the child's parent in every sense – including on the adoption certificate which replaces the birth certificate. After the adoption order is granted, the law regards the child as having been "born to" the adopter, the adopter's relatives become the child's relatives, inheritance is from the adopter not the birth parents, and so on. The partner (of the adoptive parent) with a residence order has less than complete or permanent parental responsibility. Although they acquire the right to make everyday and some important decisions about the child, alongside the adopter – including consent to medical treatment, change of name, etc – they do not become the child's legal relative, and the child does not inherit from this partner unless specific provision is made in their will. The partner will also not appear as a parent on the adoption certificate. Perhaps of most significance is the fact that if the adopter and partner were to split up and the partner leaves the family home, the residence order would be vulnerable to an application by the adopter for it to be discharged and the partner would then lose parental responsibility (and therefore the right to make any decisions) for the child.

The Adoption and Children Act 2002 provides some remedies and alternatives to this awkward position for same-sex and heterosexual unmarried couples. These legislative changes produce some helpful, although somewhat curious, consequences.

From 30 December 2005 (unless there is any further delay in implementation of the Adoption and Children Act 2002), it will be possible for same-sex couples to adopt children jointly, so that both partners of the couple appear on the child's adoption certificate as the child's parents, and they share parental responsibility for the child equally.

It will be possible to "correct" the current "imbalance" of parental responsibility between the adoptive parent and partner with a residence order by the latter adopting the child. The original adopter will not have to adopt again, and will not cease to be an adopter. Both partners will be adopters of the child, both will be parents on the adoption certificate and both will have complete and permanent parental responsibility for the child.

Whilst this is a very welcome change, there are some possible snags. The second adoption will be a step-parent adoption, not an agency adoption, with the possibility of delays and hindrances that are encountered by many step-parent adoptions, e.g. the local authority will have to report on the application (and it may not be a priority for a busy social services team); and the adopters will be reliant to some extent upon the opinion of the local authority reporter about whether the order should be granted. Step-parent adopters are not entitled to adoption support services (apart from counselling and advice), although the argument might be made that since the child concerned was once looked after and the original placement was by an adoption agency, the couple should have the same entitlement as any other agency adoptive family to support services (Adoption Support Services Regulations 2005).

Perhaps the biggest snag of all is that when the same-sex couple went to court for the first adoption order, they may not have "troubled" the child with an explanation that technically only one of them would be the adopter. In the second adoption, the child will have to know that they are the subject of another adoption application, the child's views will have to be canvassed by the local authority reporter, and the child will have to go to court for the making of the second adoption order. It is possible the child will be unsettled, if not disturbed, at this unexpected development. Whilst this should not deter couples committed to having equality of parental responsibility, great care will be needed to achieve this without undermining, at least temporarily, the child's sense of legal security and belonging to both of them.

Adoption and civil registration

It will not be necessary for a same-sex couple to "civil register" before they can adopt jointly (just as an unmarried heterosexual couple will not need to marry to adopt jointly). Civil registration gives the partners the same legal rights and obligations as those of married couples (except there is no entitlement to civil register in a church).

The Adoption and Children Act 2002 provides an alternative to step-parent adoption for married couples, which is also available to civil registered couples. The adopter who registers a civil partnership with a partner of the same sex can agree with the partner to share parental responsibility for their child. This is a relatively simple and inexpensive procedure – signing a form witnessed by a court officer – but does not require an application to court for an order. Shared parental responsibility will have a legal effect similar to that for a partner with a residence order – the partner shares parental responsibility with the adopter, and therefore the right to make decisions alongside the adopter, but it is a less complete or permanent parental responsibility than that of the adopter.

It will also be possible, if the adopter does not agree to share parental responsibility, for the partner of the adopter to acquire parental responsibility by a parental responsibility order (if the court considers such an order to be in the best interests of the child).

However, such an application made against the wishes of the adopter may not auger well for family relationships.

An agreement to share parental responsibility, or an application for a parental responsibility order, will not be available to couples who do not register a civil partnership or marry. However, as mentioned above, civil registration or marriage is not necessary for a joint adoption.

In the run-up to 30 December 2005, same-sex couples might be well advised to delay their application for an adoption order until they can do so jointly.

4 Research on lesbian and gay parenting

Although there was some opposition to the amendment within the Adoption and Children Act 2002 permitting unmarried couples (whether heterosexual or same-sex) to adopt children, much of it rested upon the erroneous assumption that having lesbian or gay parents (adoptive or otherwise) is not in children's best interests. However, there is no research evidence to support this assumption.

In this chapter, we provide an overview of the research evidence in the UK and USA on the impact on children of having lesbian or gay parents, bearing in mind the limitations of the research. We then use the research findings to present the facts and examine (and *dispel*) the myths about gay men and lesbians as parents, and recommend future directions for research.

Research limitations

There are, as with all research, some limitations to the research in the area of lesbian and gay parenting. Since not all lesbians and gay men are "out", random representative sampling of lesbian and gay parents is a challenge to methodology. This is particularly so as there are no reliable data on the number and whereabouts of lesbian or gay parents in the general population in the UK, or elsewhere.

In the existing, limited research there are biases towards surveying white, urban, well-educated and mature lesbian mothers and gay fathers, and the relatively small samples studied have been recruited through community networks. It is not easy to define groups that would be an appropriate comparison to lesbians or gay parents – and comparing them to a heterosexual parenting population does not lend greater legitimacy either, as there are intrinsic differences. As Scott (2002) indicates in her excellent review of the literature in this area:

> There are also limitations in how far the findings of such research on biologically related parents and children can be simply "borrowed" to answer questions concerning the impact on children of being adopted or fostered by lesbians and gay men (p.12).

The research on biological gay fathers and their children is also extremely limited. There are no studies in the literature that have systematically examined the impact of the sexual identity of parents on their children. Two studies (McPherson, 1993; Sbordone, 1993) show similar parenting styles and skills between gay and heterosexual fathers. Mallon's study (2004) of the parenting process in a group of 20 self-identified gay fathers found that they were more likely to endorse a nurturing role for fathers, less likely to emphasise the importance of economic support, and less likely to show affection to their partner in front of the children (Barret and Robinson, 2000; Bigner and Jacobsen, 1992).

Fears about lesbian and gay parents

Although there has been a wealth of literature about gay and lesbian parenting since the mid-1980s (Pies, 1985; Bozett, 1987; Martin, 1993; Muzio, 1993, 1996; Benkov, 1994; Bigner, 1996; Mitchell, 1996; Mallon, 2004; McGarry, 2004), the idea of a lesbian or gay man as a primary nurturing figure rearing children is still remarkable to many (Towley, 2004). Many social work professionals still hold firm to a belief system grounded in the ubiquitous, negative myths and stereotypes about lesbians and gay men (Mallon, 1999), for example, that a lesbian or gay man might abuse children, that children might be encouraged or "recruited" to be gay or lesbian, or that lesbians and gay men are not suitable role models.

Those who oppose the idea of gay men and lesbians as parents or carers base their thinking on a number of fears, including:

- that the child will be bullied or ostracised because of having lesbian or gay parents;

- that the child might become gay or lesbian because of having a lesbian or gay parental role model;

- that living with or having contact with a gay or lesbian parent may harm the child's moral well-being (these beliefs may have their foundation in religious texts that condemn homosexuality);

- that the child will be abused (based on the myth that all gay men are sexual predators).

None of these rationales are borne out or supported by evidence (Dunlap, 1996; Patterson, 1996; Stacey and Biblarz, 2001; Carey, 2005). Crucially, such attitudes can have an impact on social work professionals undertaking assessments of lesbians and gay men.

The myth of gay men as child abusers (Groth, 1978; Newton, 1978) remains ingrained in the psyche of many people, including professionals in the social work field; so much so that the idea that gay men would be "allowed" to parent seems, to some, incredible. These ideas derive from the cultural myth that men in general, and gay men in particular, are sexual predators, unable to control themselves sexually and prone to sexualise all situations.

The published social science literature (Groth, 1978; Groth and Birnbaum, 1978; Newton, 1978; Cramer, 1986; Herek, 1991) also confirms that the myth of child abuse being perpetrated predominantly by gay men is a fallacy. Paedophilia is the attraction of an adult to children for sexual gratification and has nothing to do with the sexual orientation of the perpetrator. The most recent study examining sexual orientation and child sexual abuse (Jenny *et al*, 1994), which looked at 269 cases of sexually abused children, found that only two offenders were identified as gay. These findings suggest that a child's risk of being sexually abused by the heterosexual partner of a relative is far greater than the risk of being abused by somebody who might be identifiable as being gay or bisexual.

Quality of family relations

Numerous studies show that the qualities that make good fathers, mothers or foster carers are universal and not related to sexual orientation or gender. The need for fathers to be involved in the lives of their children has been very clearly established by many (Lamb, 1986, 1987, 1997; Popenoe, 1996; Biller and Kimpton, 1997; Horn and Sylvester, 2002). The ability to love and care for a child is not determined by one's sexual orientation (Sullivan, 1995). Furthermore, the desire to parent is not exclusive to heterosexuals, but is one shared by many lesbians and gay men (Martin, 1993; Benkov, 1994; Shernoff, 1996; Savage, 1999; Mallon, 2004).

As noted by Stacey and Biblarz (2001), none of the significant differences in parenting, as reported in the research, apply to children's self-esteem, psychological well-being or social adjustment. Nor

are there differences in parents' self-esteem, mental health or commitment to their children. In other words, even though there are differences, they have not been identified as deficits. In fact, the studies have found no negative effects of lesbian and gay parenting.

A few studies have reported some differences which could represent advantages of lesbian parenting. For example, several studies have found that lesbian co-mothers share family responsibilities more equally than heterosexual married parents, and some research suggests that children benefit from egalitarian co-parenting. A few studies have found that lesbians worry less than heterosexual parents about the gender conformity of their children. Perhaps that helps to account for the few studies which have found that sons of lesbians play less aggressively and that children of lesbians communicate their feelings more freely, aspire to a wider range of occupations, and score higher on self-esteem. Most professionals would see these differences as positive elements, but some critics of these studies have misrepresented these differences as evidence that the children are suffering from gender confusion.

Finally, some studies have reported that lesbian mothers feel more comfortable discussing sexuality with their children and accepting their children's sexuality – whatever it might be. More to the point are the findings reported in a 25-year British study (Golombok and Tasker, 1996). Few of the young adults in this study identified themselves as gay or lesbian, but a larger minority of those with lesbian mothers did report that they were more open to exploring their sexuality and had at one time or another considered having or actually had a same-sex relationship.

The Golombok and Tasker (1996) longitudinal study of children brought up in lesbian households assessed the quality of mother–child interaction (primarily older children). They found that children with lesbian mothers had closer relationships with their mothers and were more likely to have a secure attachment style than those in a heterosexual family comparison group. As young adults, more reported being able to communicate well with their mother about their own relationships than did those in the comparison group.

Similarly, Chan *et al* (2000) noted that, where the quality of family relationships is concerned, research comparing various forms of lesbian and heterosexual families provides consistent evidence that children are more powerfully affected by how family members relate to each other than by family structure or parental sexual orientation.

Most children brought up in planned lesbian-led families and by previously heterosexual and now lesbian mothers have regular contact with adults beyond their immediate household, including grandparents, other relatives and male and female family friends (Golombok *et al*, 1983; Patterson *et al*, 1998).

Although most research to date on gay and lesbian parenting is based on those who are biological parents, researchers looking at gay and lesbian adoptive and foster parenting have reached the same, unequivocal conclusions. That is, the children of lesbian and gay parents grow up as successfully as the children of heterosexual parents (Golombok *et al*, 1983; Patterson, 1994, 1995, 1996; Elovitz, 1995; Tasker and Golombok, 1997; Bronston, 2004).

Since 1980, more than 20 studies conducted and published in the USA, Australia and the UK have addressed the way in which parental sexual orientation impacts on children. One meta-analysis of 18 such studies (Allen and Burrell, 1996) concluded that:

> *The results demonstrate no differences on any measures between the heterosexual and homosexual parents regarding parenting styles, emotional adjustment, and sexual orientation of the child(ren).* (p.19)

Not one study has found that the children of gay parents face greater social stigma although this cannot be ruled out given the level of homophobia in the general public. There is no evidence to support the belief that the children of gay parents are more likely to be abused, or to suggest that the children of these parents are more likely to be gay or lesbian themselves. Children will, in fact, be who they are. It is important to bear in mind that the majority of lesbians and gay men have been raised by heterosexual parents.

Becoming a parent: making decisions

There are two studies that stand out as seminal works on adoption and fostering from a British perspective: Skeates and Jabri's (1988) groundbreaking *Fostering and Adoption by Lesbians and Gay Men* and Hick and McDermott's (1999) *Lesbian and Gay Fostering and Adoption*.

Although lesbians and gay men become foster carers and adoptive parents for some of the same reasons as heterosexuals, there are some unique circumstances as well (Pies, 1990; Mallon, 1998, 2004). Unlike their heterosexual counterparts, gay or lesbian individuals and couples who wish to parent will have to give more careful consideration to how they will become a parent, and at the outset will be open to different ways of becoming a family and parenting children, for example, through adoption and fostering (Ricketts and Achtenberg, 1990; Ricketts, 1991; Colberg, 1996, 2001), surrogacy or donor insemination (Bernfeld, 1995).

Lesbians or gay men who choose to foster or adopt as single parents will face stresses more to do with single parenting than with their sexual orientation (Feigelman and Silverman, 1983; Marindin, 1997; Melina, 1998, p.292).

On the positive side, gay men and lesbians who choose to create families have the advantage of redefining and reinventing their own meaning of family and parenting, precisely because they exist outside of the traditionally defined "family". They have the unique opportunity to break out of preconceived gender roles and be a new kind of father or mother to a child (Benkov, 1994).

Future research

There is a need for a study on adoptive parents that compares outcomes for children adopted by lesbian and gay parents with those for children adopted by heterosexual parents. To our knowledge, no such study has yet been undertaken.

There is also a need for more research on gay fathers and for studies which include gay fathers who have children through surrogacy or other means.

It is also critical that research studies should have a more diverse representation of lesbian and gay parents in terms of ethnicity, education, income and nationality.

Conclusion

This chapter has focused solely on the evidence in relation to lesbians and gay men *choosing* parenthood and the effects on the children they parent. Adoption and fostering, as is so well stated by Scott (2002),

Myths vs Facts

Myth: The only acceptable home for a child is one with a mother and father who are married to each other.
Fact: Research shows that children thrive in many different types of family structure. In the UK there are increasingly more diverse types of families, as discussed in the introduction.

Myth: Children need a mother and a father in order to have proper male and female role models.
Fact: Children get their role models from many people besides their parents. These include grandparents, aunts and uncles, teachers, friends, neighbours and people in public life.

Myth: Gay men and lesbians don't have stable relationships and wouldn't know how to be good parents.
Fact: Many lesbians and gay men are in stable, committed relationships and many are successfully involved in the parenting of children. All of the evidence shows that lesbians and gay men can and do make good parents.

Myth: Children raised by gay or lesbian parents are more likely to grow up gay themselves.
Fact: All of the available evidence demonstrates that the sexual orientation of parents has no impact on the sexual orientation of their children, and that children of lesbian and gay parents are no more likely than any other child to grow up to be gay. In fact, most lesbians and gay men have been raised by heterosexual parents. Of course, some children of lesbians and gay men will grow up to be gay, as will some children of heterosexual parents. There is some evidence that children of gay men and lesbians are more tolerant and open to difference.

Myth: Children raised by gay or lesbian parents will always be subjected to bullying and rejected by their peers.
Fact: Children make fun of other children for all kinds of reasons: for being too short or too tall, for being too thin or too fat, or for belonging to a different ethnic group or religion. Children can show remarkable resilience to this, especially if they have a stable, loving home environment and parents who can support them. Because of the homophobia that exists in society, some children will experience discrimination and negative comments for having lesbian or gay parents. This needs to be acknowledged and addressed. Adults who adopt or foster children need to have worked out strategies to support their children, who will already feel different or stigmatised because of not being with their birth parents.

Myth: Gay men are more likely to abuse children.
Fact: There is no connection between homosexuality and paedophilia. All of the legitimate scientific evidence supports this assertion. In addition to the research mentioned above, of the cases studied involving sexual abuse of boys by men, 74 percent of the abusers were or had been in a heterosexual relationship with the boy's mother or another female relative (Jenny *et al*, 1994).

Myth: Children raised by gay men or lesbians will be brought up in an "immoral" environment.
Fact: The research by Cameron and Cameron (1996) is most frequently cited to support the claim that having a lesbian or gay parent impacts adversely on children. They propose that homosexuality is a 'learned pathology' that parents pass on to their children by 'modelling, seduction and contagion'. There is ample evidence to discount this "research": the authors have been denounced by the American Sociological Association (ASA) for wilfully misrepresenting research; Paul Cameron was expelled from the American Psychiatric Association (APA) and censored by the ASA for unethical scholarly practices, such as selective, misleading representations of research and making claims that could not be substantiated. Nonetheless, as Stacey and Biblarz (2001) note, bias against gay and lesbian parenting remains sufficiently strong for this work to continue to be cited in court cases and policy hearings.

...are not "gay rights issues"; the "rights" they involve are the rights of children and youth to safe and effective care, and the evidence from research is that this is no less likely to be the case where carers are lesbians or gay men. (p.15)

Numerous authors reviewing the research relevant to lesbian and gay fostering and adoption have concluded that there is no evidence that lesbians and gay men are less capable of being effective parents than heterosexuals (Cosis-Brown, 1991; Hicks, 2000; Brooks and Goldberg, 2001; Stacey and Biblarz, 2001). While more research specific to the fostering and adoption experience should certainly be undertaken, there is a foundation of evidence indicating that the sexual orientation of parents makes very little difference to outcomes for children.

While the research findings summarised here are highly relevant to the concerns raised by those opposed to the consideration of lesbians and gay men as potential foster carers or adoptive parents, further research into the specific experiences of children so fostered and adopted is clearly needed.

In summary, all the relevant research examining the impact on children of having a lesbian or gay parent shows parental sexual orientation to have no measurable effect on the quality of parent–child relationships, or on children's social adjustment or mental health.

5 Issues for lesbians and gay men when considering parenting

The focus of this chapter is the issues which lesbians and gay men face as they make the decision to become parents and their experiences as adopters and foster carers. It is based on our analysis of the existing literature, qualitative data from interviews conducted with lesbians and gay men who have engaged in fostering or adopting, and many years of clinical practice. We have quoted from these sources but all names have been changed.

As lesbians and gay men are becoming more visible in society, they are being considered more seriously as potential adoptive parents or foster carers. The increasing number of lesbians and gay men choosing to adopt or become foster carers has brought the issue of gay and lesbian parenting to the forefront. There are a number of issues that social work practitioners need to consider in order to develop a knowledge base which will lead to competent practice with lesbian and gay carers.

Firstly, it is important to recognise that lesbian- and gay-parented families differ from the heterosexually-parented family. The conventional notion of a family presumes there will be two parents, one of each gender, that they will share a loving relationship and live under one roof, and that they will both be biologically related to the children they raise and recognised legally as a family. This mum-and-dad nuclear family is the baseline model in Western culture against which all other models of family are measured, and it is assumed by most to be the optimal family environment for child development, compared to which all other types of families are viewed as deficient in some way.

This model, however, does not apply to families with a lesbian or gay parent. Usually there is at least one parent who has no biological relationship to the child. Consequently, there is almost always one parent–child relationship not recognised or protected by the law.

We need to accept the premise that it is quality of care, and not family constellation, which determines what is optimal for children's healthy development. The ability of lesbian and gay parents to provide for the social and emotional health of their children just as adequately as heterosexual parents has been documented repeatedly in the research literature and

has been outlined in Chapter 4. We must also examine our own notion of family and further learn to identify what constitutes family based on the loving bonds of responsibility that have been both intended and fulfilled, and not solely on biological, legal or conventional definitions.

Decision to explore parenting

I have always loved children, and there has always been a part of me that wanted to be a dad. As a gay man, I thought it was impossible – who was going to let me be someone's parent? And it wasn't like I could just go out and get pregnant myself and have a baby. I guess I had internalised a lot of the homophobia that I had been fed – somewhere along the way, I believed that gay people could not be good parents, just because they were gay. It made me sad. I was always close to my sister's kids, but it wasn't enough to be the really devoted uncle; I wanted to be something more for a child. One day I thought, 'Why not? Why can't I be a dad?' I could be a great dad for some child. I had a lot of the qualities that make for a great parent.

Some lesbians and gay men with whom we have worked have noted that their longing to be parents stemmed from their own positive experiences with family, and the myth that lesbians and gay men could not parent was tinged with sadness, as this man noted below:

I come from a very intact two-parent home, and family has always been the centre of our lives, and my parents – being the very good parents that they were – instilled in us the value of family. Family was always very important. When it was clear to me that I was gay, there was a sadness that I could not have children and the coming out process for me was not about people knowing I was gay, it was more about losing the idea of having children.

Another lesbian mother reconciled the desire to become a parent with living life as an out lesbian:

I came out when I was 24, but previous to that I always wanted children. I'm one of seven, all

*my siblings have lots of kids and I just always
had in my head that I was going to have
children. I just always wanted to have children.
Then when I came out I thought, I guess I'm not
having kids. I didn't really think twice about it. It
didn't cross my mind to get married and have
children. I thought I'm not doing that, I'm not
living a big lie or whatever, but that's what it felt
like to me when women got married to have
children and fulfil that parenting desire. So I just
got totally into my career and then [I got] very
active in the gay and lesbian community.
I never heard of people having children as gays
and lesbians; I never heard of that.*

Another woman echoed the sentiment of initial
sadness about not being able to become a parent, and
identified the life event that helped her see that she
could indeed become one.

*Well, it was something that I had always wanted,
actually. Probably the only problem I had with
being gay was that I couldn't be a parent. At
least that's what I thought. But that changed
when I was working in London and a friend was
there, a friend from college and she was ill. She
asked us if her son could stay with us until she
got better. Her son was just 16 months old. We
were so excited, and he stayed with us for about
nine months. When his Mum got better he went
back home with her, and at just about the same
time we moved to Bristol. His leaving left this
huge, huge void. So we decided to fill that void
by trying to adopt a child of our own.*

For many lesbians and gay men, meeting another
lesbian or gay man who chose to be a parent was a
transformative experience in their lives.

*So when my friend Ben, who was an openly gay
man, adopted his first child and I spent time
with him and his partner, I realised that I could
do it and it opened up a whole new world to me.*

As with other couples, in some cases, there was one
partner who wanted children more than the other:

*Definitely Bill felt more strongly. He said that he
couldn't live without being a parent and I felt,
well, it's not that likely, but if it didn't happen I
would try to make something else important and
that would be my life. Certainly my nieces and
nephews would be more important, which they
are to many gay people, like substitutes. But my
partner felt like he could not live without having
children.*

Choosing adoption and fostering

Gay men and lesbians are in a unique position with
respect to adoption and fostering (Melina, 1998,
p.296). Most heterosexual people come to the idea of
fostering or adoption after trying or considering
different ways of creating their own family, e.g.
infertility treatment or donor insemination. Although
some lesbians may have infertility issues, many have
tried sleeping with a man or have tried to find a
donor or have donor insemination; for many lesbians
and gay men, fostering or adoption is a first choice.

Like all potential adopters and foster carers, lesbians
and gay men have had to learn about the process.
The women and men whom we have met have been
resourceful and have gathered information from
books (Benkov, 1994; Martin, 1993), and from other
people who have adopted or fostered, including
heterosexual people as well as other gay men and
lesbians, and from agency social workers.

The issue of openness about one's sexual orientation
is an issue for lesbians and gay men considering
fostering or adoption. Also important is whether or
not they can adopt:

*We wanted so much to become parents and often
thought about and talked about adoption. We
always kept hearing how many children were in
need of homes. I thought that it would be great
for a kid who had two parents who loved them.
But I wasn't even sure that it was legally
possible for gay men to adopt.*

Many gay and lesbian prospective carers are also
concerned that agencies may offer them the children
who have traditionally been the most difficult to
place. What strikes psychologist April Martin, author
of *The Lesbian and Gay Parenting Handbook* (1993),
as ironic is that the same agencies which believe
lesbians and gay men are not suitable parents will
place with them children who require the most highly
skilled parenting. She and others have pointed out
that non-traditional families have unique strengths
that make them excellent and, in some cases, the best
homes for certain children.

In addition to understanding the mechanics of the
adoption process, it is also important to understand
how forming a family by adoption differs from
creating a family biologically:

*There was so much that we needed to learn
about the adoption process, that we always had*

to keep clearly in our minds that what we were moving towards was going to be a very life-changing event. Biologically, having a baby allowed you to prepare for nine months. Adopting a child could take nine months, a year or even more. But more than that, we were talking about a child's life here, not just this intellectual process of being a family. Sometimes that was scary, but also very exciting.

Lesbians and gay men must also decide whether to be open or not about their sexual orientation. Although foster care agencies approved single men and single women to become foster carers during the 1980s and early 1990s, most lesbians and gay men we met were determined early on, or had been warned by other lesbians or gay men who had become carers, that they should not be open about their sexual orientation. Some still opt for the "don't ask, don't tell" policy. Many gay men and lesbians do choose to be open about their sexual orientation, while others identify their partners as "friends" who will help raise the child. Despite the discomfort they feel about "going back in the closet," most take this approach as a matter of expediency, for fear of being rejected as carers. Most resent that they have to do so, but also believe it is the price they have to pay for the gift of becoming a parent.

Most lesbians and gay men who are considering fostering or adoption have probably openly identified as lesbians or gay men for some time, but as coming out is a continual process and not a one-off event, these individuals will, as prospective adopters or foster carers, experience coming out in ways that are uniquely different within their own families and communities. Becoming carers will inevitably increase their visibility within their communities in different spheres, e.g. school. This is addressed further in Chapter 7 on assessment.

Dealing with family of origin issues

Social workers will want to explore how the applicant's family of origin has responded to their desire to foster or adopt. For the lesbians and gay men we spoke to, there was some uncertainty, in general, about whether or not their families would support their decision to become parents. However, although there was a range of experiences reported and from which we quote below, the majority said their families had been very supportive.

Some families were initially shocked by their son/daughter's decision:

At first my parents were taken aback. They just kept saying, 'We don't get it, I thought gay people didn't want to have children'. They kept telling me how hard it was going to be and asked if I was sure. After they realised that we had done our homework and had given this parenting thing a great deal of thought, they were very supportive, and have been great grandparents to Tanya. I have been very fortunate I have a very loving family.

Some recalled how their parents seemed to feel the need to warn them about the realities of parenting:

When I told my father, after we had everything in process, that we were going to adopt, he first said, 'Are you sure this is what you want to do?' When I told him yes, he said, well then, great, but be prepared to give up a lot of things that you used to do for yourself. Your focus now will have to be those children.

One man recalled this heart-warming, welcoming ceremony from his family for his new son:

My family was ecstatic when Josh came. I went down that next weekend and, unbeknown to me, my entire family had assembled. They all showed up – all at one time, every single one of them. It was unprecedented – this only happened when we had weddings or funerals. I had no idea they were all gathering. When I got there, they all ran out of the house and my sister grabbed Josh and he didn't know this woman – he was being passed from one person to another. It was a very nice thing, we had a lovely dinner and it was great.

In contrast, one of the women met with complete rejection of her decision to parent by her own parents:

My family has always been so non-supportive of my life as a gay person, so it was no surprise when they were completely rejecting of my decision to parent. I told them I planned to adopt and they just rolled their eyes and said, 'Do you really think that is fair to those children?' I have dealt with the pain I feel about their rejection of me, but in some small part of my heart, I wished they could have gotten over it and been there for my children as grandparents. I think I have reconciled this pain by realising that my family is missing so much by not being a part of Joe and Jeremy's lives... they are such beautiful kids.

Whether it was assumed that parents would be supportive or not, a number of the men and women reported that they did not seek the input of their families:

We didn't tell family, not until it came time; we discussed it a little bit with siblings beforehand, but not parents. I felt, like, I was over thirty years old, and I felt like this was my personal decision and they only needed to know when it happened. It was not something I really cared for any input on from people. It was between my partner and me, and other people didn't matter, except to be informed. I didn't feel like I needed approval from anyone. It was our decision. When we did tell our families, my family was fine, but my partners' family, especially his father, were very disapproving – so much so that they didn't meet our child until he was six months old. That was hard.

Most reported that their parents approved of their decision to become parents. Many were excited by the prospect of having a grandchild. One of the first laments from parents when their son or daughter comes out to them is, 'But I wanted grandchildren!'. Their new role of parent often brought gay men and lesbians closer to their own parents. They found new appreciation and sensitivity for their parents' struggles to raise them, and they could rely on the support and guidance of their parents in raising their children. The narratives suggest that no matter how different their parenting style was from their own parents, or how different the circumstances by which they became parents, lesbians' and gay men's empathy for their parents increased when they stepped into the role of parent.

Social workers need to be aware of the strong anti-lesbian and gay sentiment held by many religious groups and the impact that this can have on family members for whom lesbian/gay sexual orientation is an issue. Families, particularly families with strong religious convictions, may openly condemn homosexuality, unaware that one of their own family members is lesbian or gay (Helminiak, 1997; Herman, 1997). Religious views of homosexuality vary widely. According to many religious creeds and denominations, sexual relations between people who are not of the opposite sex are forbidden and regarded as sinful, and many religious teaching texts have been erroneously used as a weapon against lesbians and gay men, causing a great deal of distress in many families of faith. There are several excellent resources, however, which provide an alternative perspective (Metropolitan Community Church, 1990; Cooper, 1994; Parents and Friends of Lesbians and Gays, 1997).

6 Recruiting lesbian and gay foster carers and adopters

Sellick and Thoburn observed in 1996 that 'recruiting sufficient numbers of foster carers with requisite skills and characteristics is an ongoing challenge for all agencies.' (p.44)

Ongoing concern about the supply of foster carers inevitably puts the focus on the recruitment and retention of carers. The Fostering Network estimated in March 2005 that some 12,000 new foster carers are required to meet the demand for placements and provide children and young people with the stability they need. Attention is also being paid to supporting existing carers, with a greater emphasis on providing training and support, and offering adequate compensation for carers' time and skills. Sellick and Thoburn (1996) concluded that:

> The first component of a recruitment campaign is the delivery of a clear message that foster carers are valued members of a children's services team.

Sellick and Thoburn (1996) also observed that 'the domestic and social profiles of foster carers have changed little in spite of the changing nature of foster care itself'. In considering factors in the successful recruitment of permanent substitute carers, they conclude:

> Studies make clear that a very wide range of single people or couples have successfully parented children who have experienced difficulties in their early lives or have disabilities'. (p.87)

Sellick and Thoburn (1996) quote studies by Cain (1992) and Owen (1996), both of which 'provide encouragement for the practice of recruiting new parents who are different from traditional adopters and provide useful tips on how the recruitment and support services can be improved' (p.73).

According to Boyd (2000), Helen Cosis-Brown observes:

> We have a real crisis in not having enough good quality carers. The types of people who are able to manage these children's needs are going to be extraordinary people, so we need to look at every individual who has the capacity to do this. ... My feeling is that only a tiny minority of

> adoption and fostering agencies would refuse to assess lesbians or gay men, but the ways people fail to get through the process are likely to be more subtle. I think this is because of the anxieties homosexuality provokes in some people.

With a growing number of children and young people awaiting placement, agencies are now more open to considering individuals and couples who may have traditionally been overlooked as prospective foster carers and adopters. Lesbians and gay men, in particular, are being looked to as valuable resources because they bring individual and collective strengths to the adoption and fostering task. Without preconceived notions of what constitutes family, many lesbians and gay men are receptive to adopting or fostering older children, sibling groups, and children with special needs. Many have also experienced adversity in their own lives and bring strengths to children who themselves face challenges.

What works in recruitment?

Sellick and Thoburn observed in 1996 that 'research into effective approaches to recruitment is scarce though some studies and descriptive accounts of practice provide some helpful leads'. These highlight that carers need to be valued, and recruitment messages which emphasise characteristics of carers in terms of a person specification may be more likely to attract people to apply, particularly those who may question their own suitability. In addition, they concluded that:

> Informing people about the wider package of training, financial remuneration, post placement support and possibilities of career development is therefore essential. (p.46)

Triseliotis et al (2000) concluded that:

> Powerful factors that apparently hold other people back from applying include lack of awareness, fear that they do not measure up to agency expectations, lack of confidence to care for other people's children, mistrust of social workers, the poor image of children needing care, having to return children to their families and protracted assessments. (p.65)

Word of mouth

This same study (Triseliotis *et al*, 2000) demonstrated that over half of the current carers interviewed said that they had come to hear and learn about fostering through relatives and friends or through their work, especially social care jobs. The authors concluded that 'from the comments we had, it became obvious that the experience of past and current carers are crucial in shaping a public image of fostering' (p.55). The Social Services Inspectorate's inspection of foster care services, *Fostering for the Future* (DH, 2002), reinforced 'the importance of word of mouth as the means for attracting new foster carers' (p.22).

Many lesbian and gay carers approach agencies through hearing about experiences of fostering and adoption from others within their network. From interviews with current carers, it is evident that experiences of discrimination, rejection or indifference from agencies become well known within the community and some agencies have a legacy of a "reputation" for not respecting and valuing potential lesbian and gay applicants. It is therefore important for agencies and workers to acknowledge this. Most importantly, staff members need to be comfortable working with lesbians and gay men; this includes all levels of staff – from reception to senior management.

Some local authorities and the Albert Kennedy Trust have found that having a presence at community events such as Pride* has worked well in attracting interest in fostering and adoption – and taking recruitment actively into the community has served to affirm that they value and are interested in the community. Similar lessons have been learnt in the effective recruitment of black and Asian carers.

Use of the press

Triseliotis *et al* (2000) noted that:

> *Over a third of carers came to know about fostering either through reading a feature article or seeing an advertisement in the press, mostly their local paper. Around nine in ten fostering households regularly read a newspaper... more important, over half of all carers read their local newspaper.* (p.55)

Triseliotis *et al* also concluded that television, and sometimes local radio, played a significant part in recruitment. Poster displays, leaflets and staff seemed to have less impact, though they sometimes triggered the final decision to do something about it.

Some local authorities and agencies have made effective use of advertising in the lesbian and gay press (*The Gay Times*, *The Pink Paper*, *Diva* and *G3*) e.g. the London boroughs of Tower Hamlets and Southwark and the Albert Kennedy Trust (see *Useful Organisations*) run regular adverts in the lesbian and gay press which specifically make reference to adopters and carers being lesbian or gay. Previous adverts by Tower Hamlets have included images of lesbian and gay couples with children. Efforts to recruit black lesbian and gay adopters and carers could also be made through advertising in black and minority ethnic media.

The Albert Kennedy Trust has also recognised the importance of specific advertising for lesbian and gay carers in mainstream newspapers and magazines in order to target people who are not specifically engaged with the lesbian and gay "scene" and may not buy lesbian and gay magazines. The Trust found that advertising in the lesbian and gay press attracted white, mainly middle-class carers, and it has used the mainstream media to widen its pool of carers from different backgrounds and ethnic groups.

Current carers have spoken about the impact of seeing advertising that specifically mentioned being lesbian and gay as part of an agency's eligibility criteria, e.g. on buses and billboards, and felt more confident about approaching these agencies. As one gay carer commented: 'It demonstrated to me that they must have given some thought to us being carers, that we might be valued and given a positive response.'

Many agencies do not use the terms lesbian and gay in their eligibility criteria; they may use phrases such as people being 'in a stable relationship', or 'irrespective of sexuality' – but these terms can be unclear or misleading. However, use of the terms "lesbian" and "gay" sends a powerful and welcome message to those who might want to be considered as adopters or foster carers.

Agency response to the initial enquiry

Sellick and Thoburn (1996) observed that:

---

* Pride is an annual celebratory event for lesbians and gay men and their friends and families.

The way in which applicants are greeted when they first make contact with the agency is remembered by many of those interviewed by researchers and appears to have an important impact on setting the tone for future contacts. It is clear that a less than warm initial response to a phone call or in the course of an initial interview, may well serve to discourage some potentially successful adoptive or foster parents. Those who are finally approved describe how they had to be determined and persistent and some have commented that they fear some potentially good applicants may not survive what they see as an obstacle course designed to put them off. (p.74)

This reflects the experience of many lesbian and gay carers when they initially make contact with an agency. Some have faced outright rejection and hostility; for others the experience has been more subtle, e.g. being asked early on in the phone call 'What is your husband's/wife's name?' One lesbian carer recalled having to deal with a social worker's embarrassment and confusion when she realised she was taking an enquiry from a lesbian couple:

If she couldn't deal with that, what did it say about the agency and how they would treat us? Clearly, they had not given any thought to the fact that lesbian and gay couples might apply. It also meant I had to come out in response – it did not feel positive or comfortable.

In an interview with one of the authors, Nigel and Richard, a gay adoptive couple, recounted their experience of one local authority on their first contact. They had asked about the authority's previous approvals of gay and lesbian couples and were told that they had 'recently placed a child with a gay couple. He was a child that was so handicapped that he would never know that they were gay.' Needless to say, Nigel and Richard did not make an application to that agency.

Responses to initial enquiries need to be friendly and immediate. If specific adverts have been placed, agencies need to be prepared to manage the response to advertising in a positive and efficient manner.

Information packs

Written information needs to provide clear information regarding eligibility, the task of caring, the characteristics of competent carers, and the needs of children waiting for placement. It may also be useful to include reading material and resources

that include reference to lesbian and gay adoption and fostering.

Some information packs reviewed by the authors included examples of different types of families who could foster or adopt, including lesbian and gay families.

Specific recruitment of lesbian and gay carers: points to consider

The following questions are important for agencies and professionals to consider when seeking to recruit lesbians and gay men as carers and adopters.

- Are your agency's senior management/elected members/trustee board supportive of specifically recruiting lesbian and gay carers? If not, how can this be addressed?

- What training is available to social workers, managers and panel members in relation to lesbian and gay fostering and adoption? Where can such training be accessed?

- Are gay and lesbian families visible anywhere in your agency publications? Are pictures of gay and lesbian families and black gay and lesbian families featured along with other families in agency materials, or in photographs displayed in the premises?

- Does your agency have a welcoming statement to all families? Is it inclusive of lesbian and gay applicants? Do your forms say "applicant" or "carer" or do they ask for "male and female" applicants or "husband and wife"?

- Is your training inclusive? Are lesbians and gay men depicted in case studies, in examples given, or on panels?

- What support services are your agency able to offer to families? Are other gay and lesbian parents available as mentors? Is a support group offered for lesbian and gay carers? Are staff familiar with resources for lesbian and gay families?

Preparing for negative feedback

Negative responses from politicians, religious leaders and the media have made some local authorities and adoption agencies reluctant to publicise their willingness to recruit lesbians and gay men. At a time when there is a shortage of people willing or able to parent children with complex needs, individual workers and managers need to be prepared for negative comments and develop confidence in challenging the myths and stereotypes associated with lesbian and gay parenting.

Key points

- Word of mouth is the most effective tool in recruitment, so agencies need to be aware of how they are perceived by lesbian and gay applicants and the reputation they acquire.

- It is important to use the lesbian and gay press in recruitment drives.

- It is important to also use the mainstream press, specifically using the terms lesbian and gay in eligibility criteria and advertising.

- Information packs should present information about eligibility and include images of lesbian and gay carers and information about lesbian and gay adoption and fostering, e.g. relevant books and websites.

- Initial contacts are very important. The agency's response should be welcoming and interested. Assumptions should not be made about the applicant's partners or family composition.

- Follow-up of enquiries should be immediate and friendly.

- Senior management in the agency must be supportive of recruiting and supporting lesbian and gay carers.

- Training and support should be available to managers, practitioners and panels on recruiting and retaining lesbian and gay carers.

Assessment of lesbian and gay foster carers and adopters

Deciding to adopt or become a foster carer for a child is a huge step. Potential carers are understandably apprehensive about what the process entails – lesbians and gay men, given their history, may have even greater cause for concern. Overall, there are far greater numbers than may be publicly known of lesbians and gay men who have successfully fostered or adopted, but the view that lesbians and gay men will simply be rejected is still a commonly-held perception.

It is well established that the majority of professionals who provide health and social services to looked after children and families are heterosexual (Mallon, 2000). During the past decade, various efforts have been made to enhance the ability of such professionals to respond effectively to the needs of people who are not heterosexual (Cosis-Brown, 1998; Hicks and McDermott, 1999). These efforts have been largely sporadic, with an emphasis on raising awareness and sensitivity. Additional efforts have sought to increase knowledge and understanding about the history and culture of specific groups of lesbians and gay men. These attempts, however, have not addressed the issue of effective practice in a comprehensive and sustained manner and, although a good beginning, are less than adequate. Competent practice with "diverse populations" (which has heretofore excluded issues pertaining to sexual orientation from its discussions) has become a buzz phrase in dire need of clarification if we are to move beyond the splintered approaches that have characterised previous efforts.

The challenge for professionals

There is a clear imperative for local authorities to provide effective services for prospective lesbian and gay adopters and foster carers, in order to meet the needs of children. Social work educators, as well as practitioners, often assume that competence with gay and lesbian groups can be achieved through short-term, and often "one-off", workshops or by inviting gay and lesbian guest speakers at lectures (Mallon, 1998). These assumptions reflect a short-sighted, simplistic view of a complex process. Restructuring one's views and developing a sound base of knowledge and skills should be long-term professional endeavours (Diller, 1999, p.25).

As in all professional development, there is no ideal completion point. Mallon (1998) describes the counsellor's skills in issues of sexual orientation as

A professional who begins with a well-developed sense of self-knowledge and then expands beyond his or her narrow world views to broadly include a diverse group of persons, including those diversities which pertain to issues of sexual orientation.

Thus, any serious initiative to work effectively with gay and lesbian populations begins with this premise.

As firmly expressed by others (Cosis-Brown, 1998; Hicks and McDermott, 1999), preparation for serving gay and lesbian populations effectively must be pursued on a multi-dimensional front. A unimodal focus on raising awareness or sensitivity is required but is inadequate by itself. Neither approach is acceptable to believe that increasing one's level of cognitive understanding of lesbians and gay men is all one needs to do. Nowhere is this issue more relevant than during the assessment process.

The assessment process

Agencies are required by law to carry out a full assessment of applicants before approving them as carers. The information to be collected and the required checks are detailed in the relevant regulations and standards.

This chapter is intended to assist those undertaking the assessment of prospective adopters or foster carers who self-identify as lesbian or gay.

The frameworks and concepts used to inform the process of assessment have evolved over a number of years. The earlier periods of adoption had a strong emphasis on assessing social workers being able to identify the "ideal" couple – marked by their conformity to the stereotype of the nuclear family. Marriage, heterosexuality, an active religious life, sound moral values and an unimpeachable character were some of the hallmarks of the prospective adopter. While this sounds both repressive and discriminatory by today's ideas, these features have played a significant part in the evolution of practice frameworks. While this has changed as society's values and standards have changed, others have been specific to social work and family placement practice.

One very significant change has been the emphasis on the psychology of adoptive family life and, with some modifications, the psychology of foster care. Here concepts such as loss and change have exerted a powerful influence on helping social workers understand some of the formative features in the development of human beings and particularly their capacity to become adopters or foster carers. It was a development that enabled family placement practitioners to move away from being judges of moral character to assessors of psycho-social character. It was a development that again reflected the values of its time but as important a development as it has been, the search for "psychological soundness" could be experienced as being as oppressive and discriminatory as the search for moral soundness.

There has also been a move away from the model that has treated gay and lesbian applicants as being the same as their heterosexual counterparts, to acknowledging the different experiences that being a gay or lesbian carer brings to fostering and adoption. As gay and lesbian carers have demonstrated their unique strengths as foster carers and adopters, there has been less need to argue that they are "just as good" as heterosexual carers, with the underlying presumption that the heterosexual model of family life is best.

The development of the concept of competence has also been of significance.

The concept of competence

The concept of competence will be familiar to many social workers, either through their experience as students on Diploma in Social Work training courses or as practice teachers. Competence is a three-dimensional concept which combines values, skills and knowledge in a directly observable and measurable way.

In attempting to be explicit and focusing on what people have done and can do across a range of life experiences, competence can be an empowering concept. Rather than feeling judged as a result of their life experience, or indeed their lack of experience in some areas, applicants have the opportunity to demonstrate the value of their

learning from a wide variety of situations and circumstances. In this approach, the onus is on the applicant to identify, collect and organise the evidence to prove that she or he meets the core requirements.

The active involvement of applicants in the assessment planning and in the collecting of their own evidence helps their understanding of the competences required of adopters or foster carers and encourages a commitment to personal development and training. The onus is on the assessor to ensure that the applicant understands the requirements and responsibilities, and to support and guide the applicant through the evidence-gathering process.

A framework for assessment

The development of a competency-based approach has been accompanied by the parallel development of the Assessment Framework with its complementary dimensions of Child Development, Parenting Capacity and the Wider Family and Environmental Factors (DH, 2000). While this Framework attempts to generically outline those factors social workers should pay attention to in assessing children's needs and the range of circumstances that might affect how these needs are met, it has primarily been developed in the context of children living with their birth parents or families. Its use in assessing prospective adopters or foster carers has not been thoroughly explored. In particular, it does not pay attention to the fact that, for many prospective adopters or foster carers, the assessment is an assessment of something that has not yet happened – the placement of a child born to other parents and possibly with significant lived experience with that family. Even where applicants have direct experience of looking after children, the experience of looking after somebody else's child, even as a long-term or permanent carer, is different. For the applicants and for the assessing social worker, they are trying to make sense of a future that may be radically and unpredictably different from both current circumstances or past experience. The assessment is therefore predictive of what might happen in the future but also predictive of circumstances that are likely to radically change. Predicting the future is an inexact science in the best of circumstances and prospective adopters, foster carers and assessing social workers must be very cautious about over-stating the link between past, present and future. While the past and the present are the only guide to how the applicants might adapt and respond to the future placement of a child, what exactly it is about the past and the present that tells us something of significance about the future is important to unpick. While some people respond to serious and challenging circumstances in their lives with resilience and unexpected knowledge and skill, others struggle. Social workers and applicant/s cannot be expected or expect themselves to do what is not possible. A realistic appraisal of the limitations of practice frameworks and knowledge is an important part of the competent professional.

The framework for the assessment of carers evolves through time and is responsive to changing societal values as well as changing social work values and practice imperatives. How these assessment frameworks should be judged as "fit for purpose" is difficult as there is so little research, although a great deal of practice wisdom. Currently, for instance, there is significant interest in the use of "attachment" concepts, which in part is a return to the significance of psycho-social concepts like loss and change. One study (Steele *et al*, 2002) has identified that adopters' attachment status predicts the development of the child's attachment status over the beginning of the placement. But even with important studies such as this, it must be the case that in such a complex and far-reaching process as the assessment of prospective carers, no one concept or one approach will be sufficient. With the limitations on the predictive capacity of any approach, the emphasis should be as much on providing post-placement support as on pre-placement assessment. While every effort should be made to identify applicant/s who may be unsafe or unfit to care for children or to identify potential risk factors, the strengths of people, necessarily established by evidence and supported by planned resources and services, must equally play a part.

As in any assessment, the values and opinions of the assessor can influence both the process and the outcome of the assessment. Therefore, those conducting the assessment need to ensure that they are working to an agreed set of values which will specify the spirit in which the assessment should be conducted. These values should include:

- promoting equality;
- working in a way that challenges discrimination; and
- maintaining confidentiality.

The first contact

In initial interviews with carers, social workers must be clear in their language, their affect, and in setting the tone, that they are open and accepting of lesbians and gay men as carers. Social workers must also be aware that the applicant, at this initial interview, may not be "out". Many lesbian and gay applicants will, in turn, be assessing both the social worker and the agency for "safety", trying to determine whether the agency will support them. Trust will develop over time, although some lesbians and gay men will "come out" directly at this first interview.

Jane and her partner, Rebecca, made the following observations about approaching an agency and preparing for a first visit.

I found myself with a dilemma. So far, I'd yet to ring up an agency and ask direct questions about their policies in considering a lesbian couple for adoptive parents. Now I wasn't sure if I'd asked the right questions, or been thorough enough to ensure that the agency we appeared to have chosen (or, actually, appeared to have chosen us) would have a thorough understanding of lesbian and gay issues in their assessment of us. On the other hand, there was an equal opportunities statement, and I knew through contacts that we wouldn't have been the first gay couple to be considered. I equally didn't want to draw attention to my sexuality, and highlight it as an issue – when I didn't think it should be.

I sought advice from online forums (avoiding Pink Parents, as they appeared to start from a negative viewpoint) and tried a new approach – Adoption UK. As it wasn't a forum specifically aimed at gay parents, I wasn't sure what kind of a response I would get, but it was more than just positive. It was helpful and informative, coming from people who had already been through the system, and were glad to be realistic, but positive in their assessment of their experience, and in offering advice. They reassured me that I wasn't going to spend my entire assessment period justifying my relationship or suitability to parent children.

I decided not to grill the social worker on his first information visit. My mum, however, was already concerned about the possibility that we may face discrimination in the process. Despite her threats to 'give the social worker a piece of my mind' if they dared show signs of not being willing to take us on (on the basis of our being gay), she wanted to show her support, so she was present with us when we met our social worker for the first time.

To our surprise, the social worker who turned up to talk to us about adoption was himself gay. Any doubts we had quickly disappeared, and left us feeling able to ask questions related to gay issues, without feeling we were making an issue out of being gay. My own concerns related to the potentially homophobic attitude I may experience from birth parents, rather than from anyone involved in the assessment process itself, and these fears were answered, and honest consideration given to my "what if" scenarios. Our only other concern was that I didn't want to have to make a decision about who would be the named adoptive parent when the decision to adopt jointly currently excludes us. But with the pending change in law [in England and Wales] which will allow gay couples to adopt jointly, it looks like this won't be a problem for us. Much to our horror, the issue was highlighted recently on the front page of a tabloid with the glorious headline 'Scandal of the gay parents'.

Preparation groups

Many lesbian and gay carers say they felt isolated and vulnerable in a preparation group, and some carers who were interviewed in the preparation of this book were nervous about dealing with homophobia in the group setting. All the carers interviewed recalled that they had not been prepared by their assessing social worker for the group training, either in general or specifically, in relation to their needs as lesbian or gay carers. Some carers observed that they felt that the onus was on them to "come out" at the start of the group. Jane and Claudette commented that both social workers and other group facilitators 'did not have a great understanding of what it meant to come out'.

In truth, it is likely that there will be a range of reactions in the group – from shock that lesbians and gay men would be allowed to adopt or foster, to those who are comfortable and accepting of lesbians and gay men as carers. It is not the prospective carers' responsibility to either manage homophobia from group members or to educate the group; these responsibilities lie with the facilitating social workers. In this respect, it is important that clear ground rules are set for the group, which make reference to accepting and valuing diversity and challenging discriminatory comments.

Referees

Providing suitable referees can sometimes pose a difficulty for gay and lesbian couples, as Jo and Rebecca highlight.

The only stumbling block we've had so far is providing "ideal" references. We're aware that the "perfect" referee will have known us both for a length of time and be able to give concrete examples of how we delight in going round every Friday to baby-sit for their children... Unfortunately, being gay, most of our friends – although in long-term relationships – are also gay, and equally childless. We've found this difficult, and have had to compromise, but so far, our named references don't appear to be meeting the ideals of the social worker. But I suspect this is a weakness in most applications from gay couples.

Statutory guidance and local policy and guidance will specify requirements about applicant/s' nomination of suitable referees. Where there is any uncertainty about who might be suitable or acceptable as a referee, applicant/s should discuss this with their agency.

In recent years it has been recommended that, where there have been previous significant partnerships or relationships, references should be sought. This is particularly so where these partnerships have included the care of children. This development has caused some controversy and anxiety, especially where it puts previous partners in a powerful position over the applicant/s' current circumstances. Balancing the need to explore the issue in order to safeguard children while not exposing the applicant to unwarranted intrusion or malicious accusation takes considerable professional skill and local policy and practice guidance.

The home study

Should the home study be different for lesbian and gay carers? In her article, 'Gender, sex and sexuality in the assessment of prospective carers', Helen Cosis-Brown (1992) argues that these areas are an important part of the assessment process, as

they are an integral part of our lives and how we see ourselves and are perceived by others, but they are also highly privatised areas and sometimes split off from the rest of our lives. For social workers, addressing this issue in their work can feel like crossing an inappropriate boundary. (p.12)

In terms of gender, Cosis-Brown observes that 'how people organise themselves, and experience their gender and gender relationships, will have implications for the children placed with them'. She argues that "open" family systems are more likely to offer successful placements:

If a couple are being assessed, they need to feel comfortable with the roles they have within their household, and have the capacity to negotiate change if and when that is required.

With regard to sex and sexuality,

how we feel about ourselves physically and sexually is likely to have profound implications for the development of children in our care... assessing social workers should be assured that prospective carers have a clear enough sense of their own sexuality and sexual boundaries to help children with their difficult emotional experiences, which may manifest themselves in quite problematic ways. (pp.12-13)

In his article, 'Good lesbian, bad lesbian... regulating heterosexuality in fostering and adoption assessments', Stephen Hicks (2000) observes that:

The social work assessment of fostering and adoption applicants rests upon a conflation of "sex – gender – sexuality" so that each is assumed to flow naturally from the other for heterosexual applicants. More importantly, the terms are frequently confused within social work assessments, with the result that ideas resting on assumptions about gender (who can do certain caring tasks, for example) are linked to those based upon sex (women can do certain tasks and men can do others). (p.159)

Where lesbians are being assessed, Hicks believes that

Anxieties about gender and heterosexuality are raised because the lesbian is regarded as someone who does not fit into the "sex – gender – sexuality" system, her gender roles may be viewed as suspect, she may be seen to influence adversely the gender or sexuality of children, and her lesbianism is always "different" from the usual heterosexuality. (p.166)

It is important, therefore, to consider how assessing social workers may theorise sexual orientation. For some, anxieties are raised in relation to the motivation of lesbians and gay men, their capacity to parent and their gender roles.

Specific areas to be addressed

Gender, sex and sexuality are important areas to be considered in *all* assessments. The assessment process for lesbian and gay men carers or adopters can become skewed if the assessing worker is either over-focusing on sexual orientation or totally ignoring it. Sexual orientation cannot be ignored in the assessment process, because an individual's sexual orientation is part of who they are and will impact on their life as a carer. What needs to be established early on in the assessment is the applicant's ability to constructively manage homophobia or heterocentrism in their own lives.

Helen Cosis-Brown (1991) argues that the same competency-based approach should be used for *all* applicants, but that with lesbian and gay carers the following specific areas should also be addressed.

The individual's experience of their homosexuality, their own and their family's response

Clearly, sexual orientation will be an issue to be fully and openly discussed at this point in the assessment process. Many lesbians and gay men who have been through this process have found that some social workers either unnecessarily focused on their sexual orientation too much, or conversely, did not address the issues at all. Cosis-Brown (1991) notes further that lesbian and gay applicants have spent a lot more time thinking about their sexual orientation than most heterosexuals have, and that the reticence to address this issue more often lies with the social worker.

Many prospective applicants write their autobiographies as part of the assessment process, and they may choose to address issues relating to their sexual orientation as part of this. For many lesbians and gay men, realising their sexual orientation and coming out to friends and family is a significant life event, as is meeting their partner. The autobiography should not focus on issues relating to sexual orientation, since this is only *one* part of a whole person's life experience. Neither should the applicants be encouraged to hide or downplay this aspect of their lives.

Additional questions could be considered such as: When did you first feel different in terms of your sexuality? Who did you talk to? Where did you find support?

How confident does the individual feel in relation to their sexual orientation? How comfortable are they as lesbians or gay men?
It will be important to explore with potential carers their experience of coming out, and the impact this process has had on their significant relationships within their family and community. Assessing potential carers' level of "outness" and exploring with them at what point in their development they did actually come out are an important element of practice, as is understanding the need to hide or selectively disclose one's orientation. Comfort levels with one's "outness" is a key factor for the prospective lesbian and gay adopter or foster carer, as being uncomfortable about being out can complicate the parenting process. Being comfortable with being out suggests that one has integrated their lesbian or gay sexual orientation into their lives.

Here are some questions to consider:

- At what point did you consider coming out to others?

- Are you out in the community? At work? With your family? With friends?

- Are you out to your partner's parents and extended family?

- What has been the attitude of your extended family to your partner? Have they been inclusive and welcoming?

- Is your family supportive of you (and your partner) fostering/adopting a child?

Some lesbians and gay men and their partners are cut off from their extended families because their relatives are unable or unwilling to respect their identity. Of course applicants should not be penalised because of their extended family's choices, but this information should be included so that a worker reading the assessment has a picture of the broader family system the child would join. In addition, a social worker should be available to explore what support networks are available to the potential adopter or foster carer and to their children.

- How have homophobia and heterosexism impinged on their lives? How do they feel they have dealt with this, and what present coping devices do they use?

- What are their present relationships – sexual, emotional, supportive, family, etc? How do they negotiate homophobia within close relationships, e.g. with their siblings?

- With reference to the future, have they thought about relating to birth parents, relationships with other carers, e.g. at school, playgroup, etc? How much research have they done in relation to attitudes of local institutions, e.g. schools? How would they help a child who experiences prejudice because of their (the carer's) sexual orientation?

Partnerships and relationships

There is some debate about whether social workers should ask applicants about their sexual relationships, and if they do ask, what should be done with this knowledge. Helen Cosis-Brown (1992) argues that questions about sexual relationships should be part of the assessment for *all* couples. She states:

> *Firstly, sex is a form of communication... and secondly, sex is a source of pleasure... How we feel about ourselves physically and sexually is likely to have profound implications for the development of children in our care. How children feel about themselves physically and sexually will also have implications for how they relate to others and society. This is all part of developing a good enough sense of self, and helping this development is one of the major tasks for prospective carers. (p.15)*

Carers and parents will meet with challenges in dealing with their adolescents' sexuality, and they have a responsibility to help young people think about the nature of sexuality and relationships and provide them with information about safe sex.

Some children placed for adoption or foster care will have been sexually abused; for some this will not have been known at the time of placement. Cosis-Brown (1991) observes that

> *Assessing social workers should be assured that carers have a clear enough sense of their own sexuality and sexual boundaries to help children with their difficult emotional experiences, which may manifest themselves in quite problematic ways. (p.16)*

The following questions relating to significant relationships need to be explored with all applicants:

- What qualities does each partner bring to the relationship?

- What makes the relationship positive for each partner? How do they support each other? How do they cope with stress and difficulties?

- How will a new child affect this relationship, for example, how will they cope with a child who becomes attached readily to one partner and much more slowly to the other?

- Have other options been considered and explored as pathways to parenthood?

- How are decisions made? Is there wider family involvement in the decision-making process?

- What are the strengths and vulnerabilities of the partnership?

- For how long have they been in a partnership? What are their future plans?

- Do they plan to register a civil partnership when this is available?

- Have they thought about what would happen to any child that they are caring for if they did separate?

- Have there been previous significant relationships, and if so, what has been learned from these? Do they affect the present partnership? Are there children from any previous relationships, and if so, how will those children be affected by the decision to become carers?

Other adult members of the household

This includes significant adults who live with the applicant/s as well as those who do not. What is their relationship to the applicant/s? What is their attitude to the proposed placement, and how important is that attitude to the applicant/s? Issues of sexual orientation may be relevant to discuss here.

Motivation

For lesbians and gay men, questions relating to motivation are very relevant for discussion because creating families by birth may not have been an option. Fostering and adoption is often their first choice.

Lifestyle

For lesbian and gay prospective adopters or carers, an experienced and competent worker should inquire about the prospective parents' lifestyle, but should not over-emphasise the lesbian or gay issues. In reality, most lesbians and gay men have a gay or lesbian "life", not a gay or lesbian "lifestyle". Being lesbian or gay has become a part of who they are as people, not the entire issue. Some lesbians and gay men attend gay or lesbian venues, i.e. lesbian and gay community centres, and some do not. Prospective carers may need to evaluate the way in which individuals or couples spend their recreation and leisure time.

What representations of lesbian or gay relationships do they have in their household, for example, pictures and sculptures? May this need to change?

Valuing difference

Most lesbians and gay men have experienced discrimination. Most can, therefore, understand the impact on looked after children of discrimination and being different.

Safe caring

Those undertaking assessments may make different judgements about safe caring practice in relation to lesbian and gay applicants and these should be evaluated. One social worker who had completed an assessment of a lesbian couple recently observed that it was difficult to talk about strategies for minimising allegations, as the framework for examining the issues was still "very sexist". Assumptions are perhaps still made that women are "safe" or "safer" carers than men – and perhaps these issues could potentially be minimised with lesbian applicants. For gay men, it is different, and they are vulnerable to being seen, at the very worst, as potential abusers. How can they keep themselves and their children safe and still have a normal family life? For some workers, this raises the issue of whether it is safe to place boys or girls with them.

The child in placement

How will carers discuss their sexual orientation with the child? How will they support a child in the community and address any homophobic comments they experience? How do they view emerging sexuality in adolescence, and how would they ensure an appropriate sex education? What would they include in this?

All the contributors to Hicks and McDermott's (1999) book who were involved in long-term fostering or adoption spoke about being out to their children.

> *For some this was something made clear to the child before placement, for others it was something that happened after placement. For all, it was central to their relationship with the children in their family that the children should know who they are and see that they are proud of their gay identity. Some of the children and young people knew about lesbians or gay men via characters in television soaps...* (p.167)

One carer also talked about how this can be used to explain the carers' sexuality to children or young people.

Panel

The responsibility of the adoption/fostering panel is to ensure that the assessor's recommendation is based on information which provides relevant and sufficient evidence of the applicant's ability to meet the agreed competences. The panel must then decide whether or not to endorse the recommendation.

The values and attitudes of panel members are often an issue. Recurring themes at panel with respect to lesbian and gay adopters or carers include the following homophobic responses:

- 'Where is the positive male/female role model?'

- 'Who is the mother?'

- 'How will you explain your relationship to children placed with you?'

- 'Won't you make them gay?'

Keith and David spoke of their experience at panel. 'The panel chair was very rude. He said the worst insult to a child would be being called queer. He also asked us if we thought that our children would become lesbian or gay.' Keith and David were left with the feeling that, in this instance, the panel felt they had to say something about their sexuality, but did not quite know what to say.

Andrew and Stephen, who have had a baby girl placed with them, were asked at panel about role models; one of the issues that arose in connection with this was that they would not be able to teach a girl to put on make-up. Both men work in the field of make-up and design and, as their social worker

commented, they were probably better placed to teach these skills than many women. Their social worker also observed that they had identified an 'extensive list of female role models in their support networks – and here they did more work than would have been expected by heterosexual applicants'.

Panel members can be as homophobic and discriminatory as anybody else. They should be subject to training, monitoring and equal opportunities frameworks, as any social worker. The bullet-pointed questions above are discriminatory and must not be asked. The most important question is the capacity of any applicant to meet the individual needs of any child placed with them. The sexual orientation of the child will need to be positively supported by the child's carers, whatever their own sexual orientation. This can be only broadly an issue for assessments because nobody really knows how adopters or foster carers will respond to these issues when they actually present themselves in the course of family development. Any family that has an issue with this will turn to those friends and family who support them, but should be able to turn to professional support if necessary.

Matching and placement

A number of gay and lesbian carers have found that placing social workers are very conservative in their notion of what constitutes family.

Once approved, some applicants are then rejected by children's social workers, or are offered children who are not within their stated choices (as are some heterosexual applicants), or they experience unbearably long delays in matching. Lesbians have been urged to take boys when they have stated a preference for girls, while gay men may not be offered girls even when they ask for them. While many children in care have had a troubled past, and have challenging behaviour and emotional problems as a result, there has been an unacknowledged policy of placing disabled children and children with learning difficulties and special needs with lesbians and gay men. This is gradually changing in some agencies; recently a local authority placed a healthy baby girl with a gay couple – this being their preferred placement choice in terms of meeting the child's needs.

The child's birth parents or previous foster carers may also object to the placement on the basis of sexual orientation. As Hicks and McDermott (1999) acknowledge,

> All foster carers have to deal with difficult reactions from birth parents looking for reasons to object to the placement of their child. Lesbian and gay foster carers are particularly vulnerable to such objections because of their marginal and contested position in relation to child care and it is important that agencies which use lesbian and gay carers are prepared to demonstrate full confidence in their carers and support them against homophobic reactions. (p.172)

The same issues are present in adoption, and the 1997 ruling in *Re W* (see Chapter 3) suggested that sexual orientation alone is not an acceptable ground upon which to deny an adoption.

One social worker we met recalled that, following a placement of a child with a lesbian couple, it became clear that the reviewing officer had a homophobic attitude and found it difficult to manage the meeting and talk with the couple. Reviews were rushed and hurried, and when the couple queried when they could lodge their adoption application, he stated 'When I say so'.

The other issue here is the preparation of children for placement. Preparation could take the form of a book prepared by the carers about their family which can be shared with the children. In doing so, they will provide an opening for the discussion about the carers being lesbian or gay.

It should be recognised that the family of choice for children may differ depending on their specific needs, but would need careful explanation if it excludes certain family groupings. Also, the child is entitled to have a say when of sufficient age and understanding about the type of family that he or she is placed in; it is critical that the child is given proper explanations and help in understanding their placement with a lesbian or gay family. The carers we have spoken with recalled that none of their children were well prepared for placement, let alone with a different sort of family. Terry and Peter observed:

> The preparation of our two boys for placement was lacking. Little was said to the boys directly, their initial questions to us showed a lack of preparation: they asked 'Are you brothers?'. They had no concept of what gay meant. They were shocked when they saw us giving each other a kiss goodbye in the morning. The boys were also confused about what to call us.

There are very few resources available to help applicants and social workers to address these issues. However, Pink Parents review a number of books on their website that feature children living with lesbian and gay parents. There are also accounts on their website of children and young people talking about their experiences of being parented in a gay or lesbian household. Pink Parents' booklet 13, *Making a World of Difference: In the best interests of our children*, focuses on the experiences of children with lesbian, gay and bisexual parents. It includes book reviews, advice, personal accounts, contributions by young people and interviews (see *Useful Organisations* for contact details).

Key points

- Applicants need information about preparation groups, including help with identifying any potential areas of difficulty.

- Social workers should be skilled in using a range of approaches when undertaking an assessment. They should also be aware of the limitations of what can be inferred from the current circumstances or the past experiences of the applicant/s in terms of the capacity to meet the needs of any child placed with them in the future.

- When undertaking the assessment, it is important that social workers address specific issues related to sexual orientation.

- The assessment must consider the future support needs of the applicant/s. In the case of adopters, this must include the possibility of returning to the agency for an assessment for adoption support. In the case of foster carer/s, this should be identified in their development and career planning.

- Panel members should have access to appropriate training and advice.

- Children need to be prepared for placement with families who are "different".

- Practitioners must be confident and prepared to challenge homophobic assumptions and comments from managers, placing social workers, birth family and panels when considering placements with lesbian and gay carers.

8 Supporting lesbian and gay foster carers and adopters

Like other foster carers and adopters, gay men and lesbians are interested in seeking ways to incorporate their children into their lives and help them make a smooth transition into family life. Like their heterosexual counterparts, they will at various times need support to sustain and maintain these connections. They will also want to meet other lesbians and gay men who have taken on the challenge of parenting.

Informal support

Studies outlined in *Adoption Now: Messages from research* (DH, 1999) note that informal networks are important in the provision of support for carers but that these may change as a result of the placement. Some carers point out that, once they had embarked upon adoption, their existing informal support began to diminish, particularly if there were those who disapproved of what they were doing or who found a child's behaviour unacceptable. Children coming into placement are also likely to be confronted with the need to establish new sources of informal support.

Adoption Now: Messages from research concludes from the available research that:

> *Adopters find the support of others with similar experience both valuable and acceptable although comparatively few in these studies belonged to organised support groups or had been paired with a link family.* (p.88)

Specific post-placement support issues for lesbian and gay adopters and carers

As with other carers, lesbian and gay adopters and carers should have access to post-placement support. However, there are particular factors that need to be taken into account in order to provide effective support for lesbian and gay adopters and carers.

In April 2004, the Family Futures Consortium held a one-day workshop for gay and lesbian foster and adoptive parents. One of the conclusions from the day was that:

The journey to parenthood for all parents is often complex and challenging. It is our experience that it is more so for gay and lesbian parents. Despite the liberalisation of legislation and professional practice in the field of social work, the reality is that gay and lesbian parents parent in a homophobic world and risk rejection by family, friends and wider society. For this reason Family Futures believes that it is very important that there is a clear identification and definition of the particular experience and needs of this group of parents in order that the service-providing professional world is more aware and more empathetic. The function of this workshop was to provide a starting point and forum for these issues to be addressed. The workshop was intended to provide a meeting place for parents where their personal experience of parenthood could be shared and reviewed in the context of Family Futures' experience of offering an attachment-focused support programme.

Twenty-two parents participated in the day. Various issues were identified which have implications for agencies when considering their delivery of effective support to gay and lesbian carers and adopters.

- Loneliness and isolation – overlapping issues of being a lesbian or gay parent with a child who has attachment difficulties.

- Validity as a parent and as a family – as a lesbian/gay parent how do you present yourself to the world and negotiate the world and the tension this causes?

- Rejection and fear of rejection for themselves as parents or for their children as children of gay parents.

- The perception of lesbian and gay families as second-best.

- A particular vulnerability with regard to safer caring issues.

- The issue of secrets and secrecy: 'Living with gay or lesbian parents often confused the normal message that foster or adoptive parents will give their children of "we have no secrets". For the protection of their children, gay and lesbian parents often have to negotiate with their children about who they can and can't tell about some facets of family life... gay and lesbian parents often felt confused, fearful or in a double bind about the issue of openness and secrecy.'

The group acknowledged that 'experiences of homophobia... might result in lesbian and gay carers deciding not to seek help and/or guidance from the very professionals who are employed to serve them. In this instance, the risk of carers becoming increasingly isolated and thereby depleted is of grave concern.'

The need for ongoing support and an opportunity to share commonalities and differences within a 'safe space' was felt to be essential for individuals to continue to work through their own issues and to better understand how these influence and affect the unique relationships between parent and child. While all of the participants acknowledged that things had improved, the effects of homophobia in both the personal and in the public and professional areas of life 'continue to be deeply disturbing'.

The group felt that their unique experiences of being lesbian and gay adults could contribute to their overall effectiveness as carers, given their ability to empathise with difference and cope with rejection.

Adoption and fostering professionals supporting gay and lesbian carers need to be aware of these issues and how they might impact on carers and children. The importance of peer support has already been highlighted, and agencies perhaps need to consider how best to facilitate support groups for gay and lesbian carers. There are several national organisations (see *Useful Organisations*) which might be able to help. PACE Family Therapy Services has recently received funding from the Home Office to work with gay and lesbian foster carers and adopters and has set up a monthly support group as part of this initiative (see *Useful Organisations*).

Characteristics of post-placement and adoption support services

Information and details about the types of comprehensive post-placement and adoption support services that families might require are familiar to adoption and fostering social workers and are covered comprehensively in many BAAF publications (see Argent, 2002; Lord, 2002; BAAF, 2003b; Bond, 2004; Salter, 2004).

For gay and lesbian adopters and carers, there are both general and specific issues which agencies should consider. Some of the characteristics of effective support services for gay and lesbian families are as follows.

- Post-placement and adoption support staff are available and competent to work with lesbian and gay families.

- Workers pull together information from many sources in order to assess the situation. For example, they source case records, talk with teachers and other professionals, procure specialised assessments when needed, and gather the perspectives of all family members. Workers spend extra time with families to give them a chance to fully discuss the difficulties they have experienced, and what attempts they have made to find solutions. At this stage, workers should be truly empathetic listeners so families can share their feelings with minimal interruption. Workers should also be able to identify if and when the issues in placement are related to the sexual orientation of the carer and when they clearly have no bearing.

- Workers use a range of interventions including support groups, attending meetings, and advocate for resources.

- It is important that workers help families to think about how adoption or fostering has affected their lives and relationships.

- Families need to learn about the effects of trauma and abuse, the impact of separation and loss, and have support in managing contact issues. Post-approval training is important, e.g. Adoption UK's training programme, *A piece of cake*, is highly respected, and four additional stand-alone modules for carers have been developed on the realties of placement, contact, education, and telling and life story work.

- Workers need to help adopters and foster carers to take care of themselves and de-personalise children's behaviour. 'It's not my fault!' and 'My child's behaviour is normal in light of her history' are important messages that parents can internalise through good adoption support work.

- Workers must also help adopters and foster carers to adapt to the normal developmental changes that occur for their child, i.e. adolescence. Workers must be comfortable differentiating the adopter or foster carer's sexual orientation issues from their child's developmental issues. One adopter made this astute comment about his son's developmental changes:

I have always taken such a pride in being a "good" parent, maybe I have tried too hard to be a perfect parent. My son could always come to talk to me about anything. Then, when he turned 12, it was like he was a different kid. He ignored me, he was embarrassed to be with me, and he was so bold and nasty. I was devastated. I immediately thought it was because he was getting teased at school for having a gay father. I had these notions that it was all because I was this gay adopter. Finally, one day when I was talking with a straight couple that I am friends with, who have a 14-year-old daughter, they set me straight and told me she behaved in the same way. These people were great parents and I trusted them. I realised at that point, and actually felt kind of stupid about it, that it has less to do with me as a gay parent, and much more to do with my son becoming an adolescent.

Lesbian and gay carers might be particularly vulnerable to feeling that they have to "prove" their worthiness as carers and parents in a different way than do their heterosexual counterparts. Supportive services which acknowledge the particular vulnerabilities and strengths of lesbian and gay carers, and which can help them to understand the context of their children's difficulties, can contribute to the maintenance of successful placements.

Key points

- It is important that agencies provide peer support and a "safe space" to explore issues.

- Lesbian and gay applicants should be given information and linked into support groups.

- It is important that accessible and ongoing post-approval training is provided.

- Adoption and fostering professionals need to recognise the particular vulnerabilities and strengths of lesbian and gay carers.

Useful organisations

The following organisations and support groups may be useful in offering support to lesbian and gay adoptive and foster families in the UK.

Adoption UK
46 The Green, South Bar Street, Banbury,
Oxfordshire OX16 9AB
www.adoptionuk.org
Tel: 01295 752240
Self-help support network. Members' newsletter for adopters.

Albert Kennedy Trust
London:
Unit 305A, Hatton Square, 16-16A Baldwins Gardens,
London EC1N 7RJ
Tel: 020 7831 6562
Email: london@akt.org.uk
Manchester:
Unity House, 15 Pritchard Street, off Charles Street,
Manchester M1 7DA
Tel: 0161 228 3308
Email: manchester@akt.org.uk
Website: www.akt.org.uk
Manchester Floating Support:
Angela Graham, AKT, City Centre Project,
52 Oldham Street, Manchester M4 1LE
Tel: 0161 228 7655
Brighton and Hove:
Address as registered office in London
Tel: 020 7831 6562
Email: brightonandhove@akt.org.uk
Northern Ireland:
Address as registered office in London
Tel: 020 7831 6562
Email: northernireland@akt.org.uk
Supporting lesbian and gay teenagers; fostering by lesbians and gay men.

British Association for Adoption and Fostering (BAAF)
BAAF Head Office
Skyline House, 200 Union Street
London SE1 0LX
www.baaf.org.uk
Tel: 020 7593 2000
Email: mail@baaf.org.uk
Central and Northern England
Dolphin House, 54 Coventry Road
Birmingham B10 0RX
Tel: 0121 753 2001
Email: midlands@baaf.org.uk

and at
4 Pavilion Business Park, Royds Hall Road, Wortley
Leeds LS12 6AJ
Tel: 0113 289 1101
Email: leeds@baaf.org.uk
and at
MEA House, Ellison Place
Newcastle-upon-Tyne NE1 8XS
Tel: 0191 261 6600
Email: newcastle@baaf.org.uk
Southern England
Skyline House, 200 Union Street
London SE1 0LX
Tel: 020 7593 2041/2
Email: southern@baaf.org.uk
Scotland
40 Shandwick Place
Edinburgh EH2 4RT
Tel: 0131 225 9285
Email: scotland@baaf.org.uk
Cymru
7 Cleeve House, Lambourne Crescent
Cardiff CF14 5GP
Tel: 029 2076 1155
Email: cymru@baaf.org.uk
and at
Suite C, 1st Floor, Darkgate, 3 Red Street
Carmarthen SA31 1QL
Tel: 01267 221000
Email: carmarthen@baaf.org.uk
and at
19 Bedford Street, Rhyl
Denbighshire LL18 1SY
Tel: 01745 336336
Email: cymru.rhyl@baaf.org.uk
BAAF is the leading UK-wide membership organisation for all those concerned iwth adoption, fostering and child care issues. Provides publications, training, information and advice, consultancy and family-finding services.

Colage.org – Children of lesbians and gays everywhere
www.colage.org
A US-based organisation that is the only international organisation specifically supporting young people with gay, lesbian and bisexual and transgender parents.

The D'Arcy Lainey Foundation (DALAFO)
PO Box 417, Oldham OL2 7WT
www.dalafo.co.uk
Email: info@dalafo.co.uk
Helpline: 01706 849979 (office hours)
Based in Oldham, north Manchester. Meetings, newsletter, and helpline. Provides help and support for lesbian, gay, bisexual and transgender parents. Also aims to provide an area where children of gay parents can come along and meet others in the same situation.

Fostering Network (previously National Foster Care Association)
87 Blackfriars Rd, London SE1 8HA
www.fostering.net
Tel: 020 7620 6400
Support, training and publications for foster carers. A pack of articles on lesbian and gay parenting, fostering and adoption is available for a £5 donation.

Gay Dads UK
www.gaydads-uk.org
Internet-based support group for gay men in the UK who have had children. Free service. Strong network of members who have been through similar situations and are at various stages of the coming out process. Team of moderators ensures that things run smoothly and that there is always a safe environment. Regular real-life meetings across UK so members can put names to faces.

IMAAN
www.imaan.org.uk
Email: info@imaan.org.uk
A social support group for Muslim lesbians, gays, bisexuals, transgender, those questioning their sexuality or gender identity and their family, friends and supporters. Imaan also holds monthly meetings on the last Sunday of each month in London. These meetings and other social events are used by the members to discuss issues of their sexuality, for guidance and support in a safe environment.

Lesbian and Gay Foster and Adoptive Parents' Network (LAGFAPN)
Northern Support Group:
PO Box 2078, Sheffield S2 4YQ
London Support Group:
c/o Stonewall, 46–48 Grosvenor Gardens,
London SW1W 0EB
Tel: 020 7881 9440 (Stonewall's phone number)
Email: lagfapn@hotmail.com

KISS
www.planetkiss.org.uk
Tel: 020 8741 1879
A social group made up of women who identify either as lesbian or bisexual and are of South Asian or Middle Eastern or North African descent.

PACE Family Therapy Services
Contact: Howard Delmonte
34 Hartham Rd, London N7 9JL
www.pacehealth.org.uk
Tel: 020 7609 4909
Email: hdelmonte@pace.dircon.co.uk
PACE was set up nearly 20 years ago to provide counselling, group work, youth support and advocacy for the lesbian and gay community. In May 2004 PACE received funding from the DfES to establish an adoption and fostering service which would provide: support for individuals and couples thinking about parenting or in the process of adopting a child; a facilitated group work programme for partners to explore adoption, family and partnership issues together in a safe environment with other couples; and training and information for adoption agencies.

PinkParents UK
Box 55, Green Leaf Bookshop, 82 Colston St,
Bristol BS1 5BB
www.pinkparents.org.uk
Tel: 0117 904 4500
Email: enquiries@pinkparents.org.uk
UK-wide information and advice on all aspects of lesbian and gay parenting. Quarterly magazine, helpline, publications, website, internet message boards, workshops, contacts.

Positive Parenting
c/o LGF, Box 102, Unity House, 15 Pritchard St,
Manchester M1 7DA
A Manchester-based group campaigning for opportunities for fostering and adoption by lesbians and gay men. Post is collected and dealt with at monthly meetings.

Stonewall
46–48 Grosvenor Gardens, London SW1W 0EB
www.stonewall.org.uk
Tel: 020 7881 9440
A campaigning organisation for gay and lesbian rights. Useful information on adoption and fostering on their website.
Stonewall Scotland
Tel: 0141 204 0746
Stonewall Cymru
Tel: 029 2023 7744 / 0124 837 0082

Bibliography

Ali T (1996) *We are family: Testimonies of lesbian and gay parents*, London: Cassell

Allen M and Burrell N (1996) 'Comparing the impact of homosexual and heterosexual parents on children: meta-analysis of existing research', in *Journal of Homosexuality*, 32, pp.19–35

American Academy of Pediatrics (2002) 'Technical report: coparent or second-parent adoption by same-sex parents', *Pediatrics*, 109 (2), pp.1112–19

Argent H (ed.) (2003) *Models of Adoption Support: What works and what doesn't*, London: BAAF

Asquith J, Hutchinson B and Simmonds J (2003) *BAAF Practice Note 40: Undertaking Competence Assessments*, London: BAAF

BAAF (1998) *Assessment: Points to consider*, London: BAAF

BAAF (2003a) *Practice Note 44: Assessing lesbian and gay foster carers and adopters*, London: BAAF

BAAF (2003b) *Thinking about Adoption or Fostering: Information and guidance*, London: BAAF

Baird V (2001) *No Nonsense Guide to Sexual Diversity*, Oxford: New Internationalist Publications

Barker S, Byrne S, Morrison M and Spencer M (1999) *Making Good Assessments: A practical resource guide*, London: BAAF

Barnett R C and Baruch G K (1988) 'Correlates of father's participation in family work', in Bronstein P and Cowen C P (eds.) *Fatherhood Today*, pp.76–8, New York: Wiley

Barrett H and Tasker F (2001) 'Growing up with a gay parent: views of 101 gay fathers on their sons' and daughters' experiences', *Educational & Child Psychology*, 18, pp.62–77

Barret R and Robinson B E (2000) *Gay Fathers*, New York: Jossey-Bass

Baruch G K and Barnett R C (1983) *Correlates of Father's Participation in Family Work: A technical report*, Wellesley, MA: Wellesley College Center for Research on Women

Beers A (1977) *The Tale of Two Families: Gay men and lesbians building loving families*, Springfield, VA: Adoption Resource Exchange for Single Parents

Benkov L (1994) *Reinventing the Family: The emerging story of lesbian and gay parents*, New York: Crown Publishers

Beresford S (1994) 'Lesbians in residence and parental responsibility cases', *Family Law*, pp.643–645

Bernfeld R (1995) 'A brief guide regarding donor and co-parenting agreements', in Elovitz M E and Schneider C (eds) *Legal Issues Facing the Nontraditional Family*, New York: Practicing Law Institute

Berridge D (1997) *Foster Care: A research review*, London: The Stationery Office

Bigner J (1996) 'Working with gay fathers', in Laird J and Green R-J (eds) *Lesbians and Gays in Couples and Families: A handbook for therapists*, San Francisco: Jossey-Bass

Bigner J J and Bozett R W (1989) 'Parenting by gay fathers', *Marriage and Family Review*, 14 (3–4), pp.155–175

Bigner J J and Jacobsen R R (1989a) 'Parenting behaviors of homosexual and heterosexual fathers', *Journal of Homosexuality*, 18(1–2), pp.173–86

Bigner J J and Jacobsen R R (1989b) 'The value of children for gay versus nongay fathers', *Journal of Homosexuality*, 18 (1–2), pp.163–72

Bigner J J and Jacobsen R B (1992) 'Adult responses to child behavior and attitudes towards fathering: gay and non-gay fathers', *Journal of Homosexuality*, 18, pp.173–86

Biller H B and Kimpton J L (1997) 'The father and the school-aged child', in Lamb M E (ed.) *The Role of the Father in Child Development*, New York: John Wiley & Sons

Bond H (2004) *Fostering a Child: A guide for people interested in fostering*, London: BAAF

Boyd H (2000) 'Double dealing', *The Guardian*, 3 May, p.1

Bozett F W (ed.) (1987) *Gay and Lesbian Parents*, New York: Praeger Press

Brill S A (2001) *The Queer Parent's Primer: A lesbian and gay family's guide to navigating the straight world*, London: New Harbinger Publications

Brodzinsky D M, Schechter M D and Marantz R (1993) *Being Adopted: The lifelong search for self*, New York: Anchor Books

Bronston B (2004) 'Children of same-sex parents fare well in research: early studies find positive outcomes, but more work remains', *New Orleans Times Picayune*, 14 November, p.14

Brooks D and Goldberg S (2001) 'Gay and lesbian adoptive and foster care placements: can they meet the needs of waiting children?', *Families in Society*, 46 (2), pp.147–57

Butterworths Family and Child Law Bulletin 50, June 2001, Reed Elsevier (UK) Ltd

Cain H (1992) *Unusual Adopters* London: Barnardo's

Cameron P and Cameron K (1996) 'Homosexual parents', *Adolescence* 31:124, pp.757–66

Carey B (2005) 'Experts dispute Bush on gay adoption issue' *New York Times*, 29 January, A23

Cass V C (1979) 'Homosexual identity formation: a theoretical model', *Journal of Homosexuality*, 4, pp.219–35

Cass V C (1984) 'Homosexual identity formation: testing a theoretical model', *Journal of Sex Research*, 20, pp.143–67

Chambers D (2001) *Representing the Family*, Thousand Oaks, CA: Sage Publications

Chan R W, Raboy B and Patterson C J (2000) 'Psychosocial adjustment among children conceived via donor insemination by lesbian and heterosexual mothers', *Child Development*, 69, pp.443–57

Clunis D M and Green D (2004) *The Lesbian Parenting Book*, Emeryville, CA: Seal Press

Colberg M (1996) 'With open arms: the emotional journey of lesbian and gay adoption', *The Family*, 2 (1), pp.6–11

Colberg M (2001) 'LGBT people can be particularly good parents of adoptees', *The Family*, 7 (2), 7, p.26

Coleman E (1981) 'Developmental stages of the coming out process', *The Journal of Homosexuality*, 7 (2/3), pp.31–43

Cooper D (1994) *From Darkness into Light: What the Bible really says about homosexuality* (3rd edn), Tucson, AZ: Cornerstone Fellowship

Cosis-Brown H (1991) 'Competent child-focused practice: working with lesbian and gay carers', *Adoption & Fostering*, 15(2), pp.11–17

Cosis-Brown H (1992) 'Gender, sex, and sexuality in the assessment of prospective carers', *Adoption & Fostering*, 16 (2), pp.30–4

Cosis-Brown H (1998) *Social Work and Sexuality: Working with lesbians and gay men*, Houndmills, UK: Macmillan

Cramer D (1986) 'Gay parents and their children: a review of research and practical implications', *Journal of Counseling and Development*, 64, pp.501–7

Crawford J M (1999) 'Co-parent adoptions by same-sex couples: from loophole to law', *Families in Society*, May/June, pp.271–8

De Monteflores C and Schultz S J (1978) 'Coming out: similarities and differences for lesbians and gay men', *Journal of Social Issues*, 34 (3), pp.59–72

Department of Health (1990) *Foster Placement (Guidance and Regulations) Consultation Paper No. 16*, London: HMSO

Department of Health (1991) *The Children Act 1989 Guidance and Regulations: Volume 3, family placements*, London: HMSO

Department of Health/Welsh Office (1992a) *The Adoption Law Review Discussion Paper no. 3*, London: HMSO

Department of Health/Welsh Office (1992b) *Review of Adoption Law: Report to ministers of interdepartmental working group: A consultation document*, London: HMSO

Department of Health/Welsh Assembly Government (2003) *Adoption: National minimum standards, regulations – voluntary adoption agencies, local authorities, England and Wales* London: The Stationery Office

Department of Health/Welsh Office/Home Office/Lord Chancellor's Department (1993) *Adoption: The future*, London: HMSO

Department of Health (1999) *Adoption Now: Messages from research*, New York: Wiley

Department of Health (2000) *Framework for the Assessment of Children in Need and their Families*, London: The Stationery Office

Department of Health (2002) *Fostering for the Future: SSI report for the inspection of foster care services*, London: HMSO

Diller J V (1999) *Cultural Diversity: A primer for the human services*, Boston: Brooks/Cole

Dunlap D W (1996) 'Homosexual parent raising children: support for pro and con', *New York Times*, 7 January, L15

Dunne G A (2001) 'The lady vanishes? Reflections on the experience of married and divorced non-heterosexual dads', *The Journal of Sexualities*, 4 (2), pp.121–133

Elovitz M E (1995) 'Adoption by lesbian and gay people: the use and misuse of social science research', in Elovitz M E and Schneider C (eds) *Legal Issues facing the Nontraditional Family*, New York: Practicing Law Institute

Evan B Donaldson Adoption Institute (2003) *Adoption by Lesbians and Gays: A national survey of adoption agency policies, practices, and attitudes*, New York: Evan B Donaldson Adoption Institute

Family Futures Consortium (2004) *One-day Workshop for Gay and Lesbian Adoptive and Foster Parents*, 25 April 2004, unpublished paper

Feigelman W and Silverman A (1983) *Chosen Children: New patterns of adoptive relationships*, New York: Praeger

Flaks D K, Ficher I, Masterpasqua F and Joseph G (1995) 'Lesbians choosing motherhood: a comparative study of lesbian and heterosexual parents and their children', *Developmental Psychology*, 31 (1), pp.105–114

Frommer M S (1996) 'The right fit: a gay man's quest for fatherhood', *The Family*, 2 (1), pp.12–16, 26

Garner A (2004) *Families like Mine: Children of gay parents tell it like it is*, New York: Harper Collins

Gay Rights Project/American Civil Liberties Union (1999) www.aclu.org

Gay Times (1997) *Special issue: Gay men and children*, Issue 225, June

Golombok S, Spencer A and Rutter M (1983) 'Children in lesbian and single-parent households: psychosexual and psychiatric appraisal', *Journal of Child Psychology and Psychiatry*, 24 (4), pp.551–72

Golombok S and Tasker F (1996) 'Do parents influence the sexual orientation of their children? Findings from a longitudinal study of lesbian families', *Developmental Psychology*, 32 (1), pp.3–11

Golombok S, Tasker F and Murray C (1997) 'Children raised in fatherless families from infancy: family relationships and the socioemotional development of children of lesbian and single heterosexual mothers', *Journal of Child Psychology and Psychiatry* 38, pp.783–91

Gooding C (1992) *Trouble and the law? A legal handbook for lesbians and gay men*, London: The Gay Men's Press

Green J (1999) *The Velveteen Father: An unexpected journey to parenthood*, New York: Villard

Green R, Mandel J B, Hotvedt M E, Gray J and Smith L (1986) 'Lesbian mothers and their children: a comparison with solo parent heterosexual mothers and their children', *Archives of Sexual Behavior*, 15 (2), pp.167–84

Greene B (1994) 'Lesbian and gay sexual orientations: implications for clinical training, practice and research', in Greene B and Herek G M (eds) *Lesbian and Gay Psychology: Theory, research, and clinical applications*, Thousand Oaks, CA: Sage Publications

Griffin K and Mulholland L A (eds.) *Lesbian Motherhood in Europe*, London: Cassell

Groocock V (1995) *Changing our Lives: Lesbian passions, politics, priorities*, London: Cassell

Groth A N (1978) 'Patterns of sexual assault against children and adolescents', in Burgess A W, Groth A N, Holmstrom L L and Sgroi S M (eds) *Sexual Assault of Children and Adolescents*, Lexington, MA: Lexington Books

Groth A N and Birnbaum H J (1978) 'Adult sexual orientation and attraction to underage persons', *Archives of Sexual Behavior*, 7 (3), pp.175–81

Feigelman W and Silverman A (1983) *Chosen Children: New patterns of adoptive relationships*, New York: Praeger

Harne L and Rights of Women (1997) *Valued Families: The lesbian mother's legal handbook*, revised and updated, London: The Women's Press

Helminiak D A (1997) *What the Bible Really Says About Homosexuality*, San Francisco: Alamo Square Press

Herek G M (1991) 'Stigma, prejudice and violence against lesbians and gay men', in Gonsiorek J C and Weinrich J D (eds) *Homosexuality: Research implications for public policy*, Newbury Park: Sage Publications

Herman D (1997) *The Anti-Gay Agenda: Orthodox vision and the Christian right*, Chicago: University of Chicago Press

Hicks S (1996) 'The "last resort?" Lesbian and gay experiences of the social work assessment', *Practice*, 8 (2), pp.15–24

Hicks S (1997) 'Taking the risk? Assessing lesbian and gay carers', in Kermshall H and Pritchard J (eds.) *Good Practice in Risk Assessment and Risk Management 2: Protection, rights, and responsibilities*, London: Jessica Kingsley Publishers

Hicks S (2000) 'Good lesbian, bad lesbian: regulating heterosexuality in fostering and adoption assessments', *Child & Family Social Work*, 5 (2), pp.157–68

Hicks S and McDermott J (eds) (1999) *Lesbian and Gay Fostering and Adoption: Extraordinary yet ordinary*, London: Jessica Kingsley Publishers

Horn W F and Sylvester T (2002) *Father Facts* (4th edition), Lancaster, PA: National Fatherhood Initiative

Hosley C A and Montemayor R (1997) 'Fathers and adolescents', in Lamb M E (ed.) *The Role of the Father in Child Development*, New York: John Wiley and Sons

Howey N, Samuels E, Cammermeyer M and Savage D (2000) *Out of the Ordinary: Essays on growing up with gay, lesbian, and transgender parents*, New York: Stonewall Inn Editions

Hunter J and Schaecher R (1987) 'Stresses on lesbian and gay adolescents in schools', *Social Work in Education*, 9 (3), pp.180–8

Ivaldi G (2000) *Surveying Adoption*, London: BAAF

Javaid G A (1993) 'The children of homosexual and heterosexual single mothers', *Child Psychiatry and Human Development*, 23 (4) pp.235–48

Jenny C, Roesler T A and Poyer K L (1994) 'Are children at risk for sexual abuse by homosexuals?', *Pediatrics*, 94 (1), pp.41–4

Jivani A (1997) *It's Not Unusual: A history of lesbian and gay Britain in the twentieth century*, London: Michael O'Mara Books/BBC

Lamb M E (ed.) (1986) *The Father's Role: Applied perspectives*, New York: John Wiley and Sons

Lamb M E (ed.) (1987) *The Father's Role: Cross cultural perspectives*, Hillsdale, NJ: Erlbaum

Lamb M E (1997) 'The development of father–infant relationships', in Lamb M E (ed.) *The Role of the Father in Child Development*, New York: John Wiley and Sons

LeVay S (1994) *The Sexual Brain*, Boston: MIT Press

Levy E F (1992) 'Strengthening the coping resources of lesbian families', *Families in Society*, 73 (1), pp.23–31

Lewis K G (1980) 'Children of lesbians: their point of view', *Social Work*, 25 (3), p.198

Lord J (2002) *Adopting a Child: A guide for people interested in adoption* (6th edition), London: BAAF

Mallon G P (1998) 'Lesbians and gay men as foster and adoptive parents', in Mallon G P *Let's Get this Straight: A gay and lesbian affirming approach to child welfare*, New York: Columbia University Press

Mallon G P (1999) *Let's Get this Straight: A gay and lesbian affirming approach to child welfare*, New York: Columbia University Press

Mallon G P (2000) 'Gay men and lesbians as adoptive parents' *Journal of Gay and Lesbian Social Services*, 11 (4), pp.1–21

Mallon G P (2004) *Gay Men Choosing Parenthood*, New York: Columbia University Press

Marchant C (1992) 'Adoption shake up avoids blanket ban', *Community Care*, October, p.1

Marindin H (ed.) (1998) *Handbook for Single Adoptive Parents*, Mount Hermon, California: National Council for Single Adoptive Parents

Martin A (1993) *The Lesbian and Gay Parenting Handbook: Creating and raising our families*, New York: Harper Perennial

Mayfield W (2001) 'The development of an internalized homonegativity inventory for gay men', *Journal of Homosexuality*, 41 (2), pp.53–76

McGarry K (2004) *Fatherhood for Gay Men: An emotional and practical guide to becoming a gay dad*, New York: Haworth Press

McPherson D (1993) *Gay Parenting Couples: Parenting arrangements, arrangement satisfaction, and relationship satisfaction*, unpublished doctoral dissertation, Pacific Graduate School of Psychology

Melina L R (1998) *Raising Adopted Children*, New York: Quill

Metropolitan Community Church (1990) *Homosexuality Not a Sin, Not a Sickness: What the Bible does and does not say*, Los Angeles: Metropolitan Community Church

Mitchell V (1996) 'Two moms: contribution of the planned lesbian family and the deconstruction of gendered parenting', in Laird J and Green R-J (eds) *Lesbians and Gays in Couples and Families: A handbook for therapists*, San Francisco: Jossey-Bass Publishers

Morales E S (1989) 'Ethnic minority families and minority gays and lesbians', *Marriage and Family Review*, 14, pp.217–39

Morgan P (2002) *Children as Trophies? Examining the evidence on same-sex parenting*, London: Christian Institute

Muzio C (1993) 'Lesbian co-parenting: on being/being the invisible (m)other', *Smith College Studies in Social Work*, 63 (3), pp.215–29

Muzio C (1996) 'Lesbians choosing children: creating families, creating narratives', in Laird J and Green R-J (eds) *Lesbians and Gays in Couples and Families: A handbook for therapists*, San Francisco: Jossey-Bass Publishers

Nelson N (1997) *When gay and lesbian people adopt*, Seattle, WA: Northwest Adoption Exchange

Newton D E (1978) 'Homosexual behavior and child molestation: a review of the evidence', *Adolescence*, 13, pp.205–15

Nicholson W D and Long B C (1990) 'Self-esteem, social support, internalized homophobia, and coping strategies of HIV+ gay men', *Journal of Consulting and Clinical Psychology*, 58 (6), pp.873–6

Owen R (1996) *Novices, Old Hands, and Professionals*, London: BAAF

Parents & Friends of Lesbians and Gays (1997) *Beyond the Bible: Parents, families and friends talk about religion and homosexuality*, Washington, DC: Parents & Friends of Lesbians and Gays

Patterson C J (1992) 'Children of gay and lesbian parents', *Child Development*, 63, pp.1025–42

Patterson C J (1994) 'Lesbian and gay couples considering parenthood: an agenda for research, service and advocacy', in Kurdek L A (ed.) *Social Services for Gay and Lesbian Couples*, New York: Harrington Park Press

Patterson C J (1995) 'Lesbian mothers, gay fathers, and their children', in Augelli A R D and Patterson C J (eds) *Gay, Lesbian, and Bisexual Identities over the Lifespan*, Oxford: Oxford University Press

Patterson C J (1996) 'Lesbian mothers and their children: findings from the Bay area families study' in Laird J and Green R-J (eds) *Lesbians and Gays in Couples and Families: A handbook for therapists*, San Francisco: Jossey-Bass Publishers

Patterson C J, Hurt S and Mason C D (1998) 'Families of the lesbian baby-boom: children's contact with grandparents and other adults', *American Journal of Orthopsychiatry*, 68, pp.390–99

Pavao J M (2003) *The Family of Adoption*, Boston, MA: Beacon

Performance Innovation Unit (PIU) (2000) *Prime Minister's Review of Adoption*, London: HMSO or The Stationery Office

Pies C (1985) *Considering Parenthood: A workbook for lesbians*, San Francisco: Spinsters/Aunt Lute

Pies C (1990) 'Lesbians and the choice to parent', in Bozett F W and Sussman M B (eds.) *Homosexuality and Family Relations*, New York: Harrington Park Press

Pink Parents Magazine Special Edition (2004) *Choosing Our Families – Adoption and Fostering*, Issue 14, March

Popenoe D (1996) *Life without Father*, New York: Free Press

Quinton D, Rushton A, Dance C and Mayes D (1998) *Joining New Families: A study of adoption and fostering in middle childhood*, Bristol: University of Bristol and the Institute of Psychiatry

Ricketts W (1991) *Lesbians and Gay Men as Foster Parents*, Portland, MN: University of Southern Maine

Ricketts W and Achtenberg R A (1987) 'The adoptive and foster gay and lesbian parent', in Bozett F W (ed.) *Gay and Lesbian Parents*, New York: Praeger Press

Ricketts W and Achtenberg R A (1990) 'Adoption and foster parenting for lesbians and gay men: creating new traditions in family', *Marriage and Family Review*, 14 (3/4), pp.83–118

Rushton A, Dance C, Quinton D and Mayes D (2001) *Siblings in Late Permanent Placements*, London: BAAF

Ryan S D (2000) 'Examining social workers' placement recommendations of children with gay and lesbian adoptive parents', *Families in Society*, 81 (5), 517–28

Salter A N (2004) *The Adopter's Handbook: Information, resources and services for adoptive parents*, 2nd edn, London: BAAF

Savage D (1999) *The Kid (What happened after my boyfriend and I decided to go get pregnant)*, New York: Dutton

Savin-Williams R C and Rodriguez R G (1993) 'A developmental clinical perspective on lesbian, gay male and bisexual youth', in Gullotta T P, Adams G R and Montemayor R (eds) *Adolescent Sexuality: Advances in adolescent development*, Volume 5, Newbury Park, CA: Sage Publications

Sbordone A J (1993) *Gay Men Choosing Fatherhood*, unpublished doctoral dissertation, Department of Psychology, City University of New York

Scott S (2002) *Research Briefing: The impact on children of having lesbian or gay parents*, London: Barnardo's

Sellick C and Thoburn J (1996) *What Works in Family Placement?*, London: Barnardo's

Shernoff M (1996) 'Gay men choosing to be fathers', in Shernoff M (ed.) *Human Services for Gay People: Clinical and community practice*, New York: Harrington Park

Shidlo A (1994) 'Internalized homophobia: conceptual and empirical issues in measurement', in Greene B and Herek G M (eds) *Psychological Perspectives on Lesbian and Gay Issues: Vol. 1 Lesbian and Gay Psychology: Theory, research, and clinical applications*, Thousand Oaks, CA: Sage Publications

Skeates J and Jabri D (eds) (1988) *Fostering and Adoption by Lesbians and Gay Men*, London: London Strategic Policy Unit

Snow J E (2004) *How it Feels to have a Gay or Lesbian Parent: A book by kids for kids of all ages*, New York: Harrington Park Press

Stacey J and Biblarz T (2001) '(How) Does the sexual orientation of parents matter?', *American Sociological Review*, 66, pp.159–83

Steele M, Steele H and Johansson M (2002) 'Maternal predictors of children's social cognition: an attachment perspective', *Journal of Child Psychology and Psychiatry*, 43, 7, pp.189–98

Sullivan A (ed.) (1995) *Issues in Gay and Lesbian Adoption: Proceedings of the Fourth Annual Pierce-Warwick Adoption Symposium*, Washington, DC: Child Welfare League of America

Tasker F L and Golombok S (1995) 'Adults raised as children in lesbian families', *American Journal of Orthopsychiatry*, 65 (2) pp.203–15

Tasker F L and Golombok S (1997) *Growing Up in a Lesbian Family: Effects on child development*, New York: Guilford Press

The Times (1997) 'Lesbian couple can adopt a child', 21 May

Towley B (2004) 'Local row breaks out over gay adoption stance', www.Gay.com, downloaded 22 November 2004

Triseliotis J, Borland M and Hill M (2000) *Delivering Foster Care*, London: BAAF

Triseliotis J, Sellick C and Short R (1995) *Foster Care: Theory and practice*, London: BT Batsford Ltd

Triseliotis J, Shireman J and Hundley M (1997) *Adoption: Theory, policy and practice*, London: Cassell

Troiden R R (1979) 'Becoming homosexual: a model of gay identity acquisition', *Psychiatry*, 42, pp.362–73

Troiden R R (1993) 'The formation of homosexual identities', in Garnets L D and Kimmel D G (eds.) *Psychological Perspectives on Lesbian and Gay Male Experiences*, New York: Columbia University Press

Turner C S (1999) *Adoption Journeys: Parents tell their stories*, Ithaca, New York: McBooks Press

The Urban Institute (2003) *Gay and Lesbian Families in the Census: Couples with children*, Washington, DC: The Urban Institute

Walters K L (1998) 'Negotiating conflicts in allegiances among lesbian and gays of color: reconciling divided selves and communities', in Mallon G P (ed.) *Foundations of Social Work Practice with Lesbian and Gay Persons*, New York: Haworth Press

Waterhouse S and Brocklesby E (2001) 'Placement choice in temporary foster care: a research study', *Adoption & Fostering*, 25:3, pp.112–18

Waugh P (1997) 'Adoption ban on gay couples', *London Evening Standard*, 27 October, p.12

Weinberg G (1973) *Society and the Healthy Homosexual*, Garden City, New York: Doubleday

Weston K (1991) *Families We Choose: Gay and lesbian kinship*, New York: Columbia University Press

Williams H A (1975) 'Problems of homosexuality', *British Medical Journal*, 16, pp.122–31